The sixth book in the Master Thinking Skills series is designed to provide students with the background that they need to enter the upper levels of their education. They expand their vocabularies by studying prefixes and roots and practice using new words in context. In addition, they continue studying newspapers and other resources that provide valuable background information for papers and biographical reports. They also learn about writing to inform, entertain and persuade and they study the difference between fact and opinion. The final unit provides tips to use while taking a variety of tests.

Table of Contents

Learning New Words 3, 4, 5, 6, 7, 8, 9
Review 10, 18, 26, 34, 42, 50, 58, 64
Using New Words...11, 12, 13, 14, 15, 16, 17
Locating Information 19, 20, 21, 22, 23, 24, 25
Using Newspapers for Research 27, 28, 29, 30, 31, 32, 33
Doing Biographical Research 35, 36, 37, 38, 39, 40, 41
Determining the Author's Purpose..................................43, 44, 45, 46, 47, 48, 49
Fact or Opinion? 51, 52, 53, 54, 55, 56, 57
Preparing For and Taking Tests.....................................59, 60, 61, 62, 63
Enrichment Preview 65-72

D1512606

Glossary

Biography. A written history of a person's life.

Chapter. Parts into which some books are divided.

Entertain. To hold the attention of or to amuse someone.

Fact. Something that can be proven.

Index. An alphabetical listing of names, topics and important words found in the back of a book.

Inform. To give factual information.

News digest. A book that contains summaries of news events.

Newspaper. A publication regularly printed and distributed, usually daily or weekly, containing news, opinions, advertisements and other information of general interest.

Opinion. A belief not necessarily based on facts.

Prefix. A syllable at the beginning of a word that changes its meaning.

Root word. A word on which longer words are based.

Table of contents. A listing of headings and page numbers for chapters or articles located in the front of a book or magazine.

Units. Parts into which some books are divided.

Name: _____

Learning New Words

Many words in the English language are combinations of two Greek words or two Latin words. If you know what part of a word means, then you may be able to figure out the meaning of the rest of the word.

For example, if **cycle** means "circle or wheel" and **bi** means "two," then you can figure out that **bicycle** means "two wheels."

Root words are the words that longer words are based on. For example, **duct**, which means to lead, is the root of **conduct** or **induct**.

Look at the chart below. It has several root words and their meanings on it.

Root	Meaning	Example	Definition
act	to do	interact	to act with others
aqua	water	aquatint	dyed water
auto	self	automobile	to move oneself
centi	a hundred	centennial	one hundred years
cycle	circle, wheel	bicycle	having two wheels

Directions: After reading about root words, follow the instructions. Look at each word in the equations below. The meaning of one part of the word is shown in parentheses. To find the meaning of the other part of the word, consult the chart of root words. Write the meaning in the blank. Combine the two meanings as shown. Look up the definition in the dictionary and write it in the space provided. Of course, the dictionary definition is more complete. But do you see how the meanings of the parts of each word figure into the definition?

1. react re (again) + act _____to do_____ = ___again to do___

   Dictionary definition: ___To act or do again_____

2. automatic auto _____ + matic (having a mind) = _____

   Dictionary definition: _____

3. transact trans (across) + act _____ = _____

   Dictionary definition: _____

4. centimeter centi _____ + meter (meter) = _____

   Dictionary definition: _____

5. recycle re (again) + cycle _____ = _____

   Dictionary definition: _____

6. aquanaut aqua _____ + naut (sailor) = _____

   Dictionary definition: _____

Name: _____

Learning New Words

Root	Meaning	Example	Definition
chrom	color	monochrome	of one color
cracy	government	democracy	government by people
equi	equal, even	equated	made equal
hemo	blood	hemoglobin	a part of blood
junct	join	adjunct	to join another thing
tend	to stretch	extend	to stretch far
tract	draw or pull	retract	to pull back
vita	life	vitality	to have life

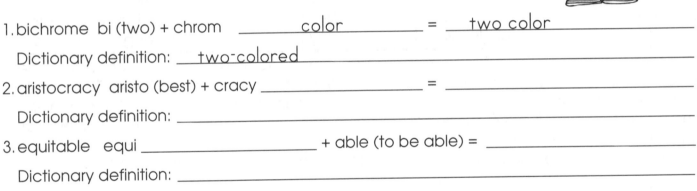

Directions: After looking at the chart of root words and their meanings, look at each equation. The meaning of one part of the word is shown in parentheses. Find the meaning of the root on the chart. Write that meaning in the blank. Then combine the two meanings. Look up the word in the dictionary and write its meaning in the space below.

1. bichrome bi (two) + chrom _____color_____ = ___two color_____

   Dictionary definition: ___two-colored_____

2. aristocracy aristo (best) + cracy _____ = _____

   Dictionary definition: _____

3. equitable   equi _____ + able (to be able) = _____

   Dictionary definition: _____

4. hemophilia   hemo _____ + philia (defect) = _____

   Dictionary definition: _____

5. disjunct   dis (apart) + junct _____ = _____

   Dictionary definition: _____

6. vitalize   vitale _____ + ize (to make) = _____

   Dictionary definition: _____

7. subtract   sub (under) + tract _____ = _____

   Dictionary definition: _____

8. distend   dis (to separate) + tend _____ = _____

   Dictionary definition: _____

Name: _____

Learning New Words From Their Prefixes And Roots

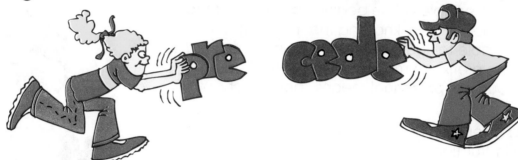

Root	Meaning	Example	Definition
cede	to go	supercede	to go beyond
cept	seize	intercept	to seize during
duce	lead	deduce	to find the lead
fere	carry	interfere	to carry into
port	carry	transport	to carry across
spect	to look	inspect	to look in
tain	to hold	obtain	to gain or by action
vene	to come	convene	to come to start

Directions: After looking at the chart of root words and their meanings, look at each word below. The meaning of one part of the word is shown in parentheses. Find the meaning of the other part on the chart. Write it in the blank. Combine the two meanings. Look up the word in the dictionary and write it in the space provided.

1. precede pre (before) + cede ___to go___ = ___before to go_____
   Dictionary definition: _to be, go or come ahead_____

2. report re (again) + port _____ = _____
   Dictionary definition: _____

3. intervene inter (between) + vene _____ = _____
   Dictionary definition: _____

4. induce in (in) + duce _____ = _____
   Dictionary definition: _____

5. retrospect retro (again) + spect _____ = _____
   Dictionary definition: _____

6. refer re (again) + fere _____ = _____
   Dictionary definition: _____

7. retain re (again) + tain _____ = _____
   Dictionary definition: _____

8. concept con (with) + cept _____ = _____
   Dictionary definition: _____

Name: _____

Learning New Words

A prefix is a syllable at the beginning of a word that changes its meaning. By knowing the meaning of a prefix, you may be able to figure out the meaning of a word. For example, the prefix **pre** means "before." That could help you figure out that **preschool** means "before school."

Directions: After reading about prefixes and their roots, follow the instructions.

A. Look at each word. Write its prefix and its base word. The prefixes **a-, im-, in-, non-,** and **un** mean "not."

Word	Prefix	Base Word
amoral	a⁻	moral
impractical	_____	_____
indirect	_____	_____
nonsense	_____	_____
unaffected	_____	_____

B. Use a word from the chart above to complete each sentence.

1. A person who does not have good ethics is sometimes called _____

2. If two sailors went through a storm at sea and

   survived, they could be _____ by it.

3. A comedian who makes many jokes sometimes talks _____

4. To carry an umbrella on a sunny day is _____

5. Buying flowers is an _____ way of saying, "I love you."

Name: _____

Learning New Words

Directions: The prefixes **co-, col-, com-, con-,** and **cor-** mean "with or together." The prefixes **anti-, contra-** and **ob-** mean "against." Use that information to complete the exercises below.

A. Read each word. Write its prefix and base word in the space provided.

Word	Prefix	Base Word
coexist	co⁻	exist
concurrent	_____	_____
correlate	_____	_____
codependent	_____	_____
antigravity	_____	_____
contraband	_____	_____

B. Use the words above to complete the sentences.

1. When airplanes fly very high and then quickly drop down, they cause an _____ affect.

2. Materials that are illegal are called _____ .

3. A dog and a cat can _____ in the same house if they get along well.

4. Events that happen at the same time are _____ .

5. When two people rely on each other, they are said to be _____ .

6. The text book will _____ with the teacher's lectures.

Learning New Words

Directions: The prefixes **epi-, hyper-, over-** and **super-** mean "above or over." The prefixes **under-** and **sub-** mean "under." Follow the instructions for each question.

A. Read each word. Write its prefix and base word in the space provided.

Word	Prefix	Root
hyperactive	hyper-	active
overanxious	_____	_____
superimpose	_____	_____
epilogue	_____	_____
underestimate	_____	_____
subordinate	_____	_____

B. Use the words above to complete the following sentences.

1. A photographer could _____ one image on top of another.

2. The _____ of the book may tell additional information about the story.

3. All the other children settled down for the night, except the boy who was _____ .

4. He could not sleep because he was _____ about the upcoming trip.

5. The company's president told his _____ to take over some of the responsibilities.

6. Just because you think you are weak, don't_____ how strong you could be.

Name: _____

Learning New Words

Directions: Some prefixes are related to numbers. For example, in Latin **uni** means "one." The prefix **mono** means "one" in Greek.

Look at the chart below. It lists prefixes for numbers one through ten from both the Latin and Greek languages

Number	Latin	Example	Greek	Example
1	uni	university	mon, mono	monopoly
2	du	duplex	di	digress
3	tri	tricycle	tri	tricycle
4	quad	quadrant	tetro	tetrameter
5	quin	quintuplets	penta	pentagon
6	sex	sexennial	hex	hexagon
7	sept	September	hept	heptagon
8	oct	October	oct	octagon
9	nov	November	enne	ennead (group of nine)
10	dec	decade	dec	decade

Look at each word in the equation below. The meaning of one part of the word is shown in parentheses. To find the meaning of the other part of the word, consult the chart. Write the meaning in the blank. Combine the two meanings as shown in the example. Look up the definition in the dictionary and write it in the space provided.

1. unicycle uni _____ + cycle (wheel) = _____
   Dictionary definition: _____

2. monogram mono _____ + gram (writing) = _____
   Dictionary definition: _____

3. sextet sex _____ + tet (group) = _____
   Dictionary definition: _____

4. quad quad _____ + rant (part) = _____
   Dictionary definition: _____

5. hexagonal hex _____ + agonal (angle) = _____
   Dictionary definition: _____

6. trialogue tri _____ + alogue (to speak) = _____
   Dictionary definition: _____

7. octave oct _____ + ave (to have) = _____
   Dictionary definition: _____

8. decigram dec _____ + gram (gram) = _____
   Dictionary definition: _____

Name: _____

Review

Directions: Read each question. Follow the instructions.

A. Look at the box of the roots and the prefixes with their meanings. Then look at each equation. Write the meaning of each part of the word in the space provided. Then combine the meanings. Look up the word in a dictionary. Write its meaning.

Roots	Meanings	Prefixes	Meanings
fere	carry	dis	separate
graph	to write	epi	upon, above
rupt	break	ex	out
tend	stretch	in	in
vade	to go	trans	across

1. invade in ____in____ + vade __to go__ = ___in to go___

   Definition: ___to go in_____

2. disrupt dis _____ + rupt _____ = _____

   Definition: _____

3. transfer trans _____ + fere _____ = _____

   Definition: _____

4. extend ex _____ + tend _____ = _____

   Definition: _____

5. epigraph epi _____ + graph_____ = _____

   Definition: _____

B. The prefixes **mono-** and **uni-** both mean "one." Look at each word. Write its prefix and its root in the space provided. Then complete each sentence with one of the words from the chart.

Word	Prefix	Root
monorhyme	_____	_____
monosyllable	_____	_____
unilingual	_____	_____
uniparental	_____	_____

1. We went on a camping trip with my father. _____

2. The Mexican children were _____.

3. Words at the ends of each line that sound similar. _____

4. "Cat" is an example of a _____

Using New Words

version	— a description or account of a particular point of view
culture	— the customs, beliefs and ways of living that belong to a group of people
triumphant	— victorious or successful
significance	— importance
tradition	— ideas, customs and beliefs passed down to other generations
bestowed	— given as a gift
historical	— relating to history
sacred	— devoted exclusively to one use

Directions: Study the vocabulary words and their meanings. Then complete each sentence.

1. Earthball is the American _____ of a game that originated in Japan.

2. The annual Japanese game of "hakozaki-gu no Tama-seseri" is a _____ event in that country.

3. It started when two balls were found floating on water and were taken to the Hakozaki shrine. Supposedly, all who touched the balls were to have happiness

_____ upon them.

4. It is part of Japanese _____ that each year two teams compete with each other for the ball on Jan. 3.

5. The ball used by the Japanese for the event is wooden and _____ , according to historians.

6. The _____ has been going on for several years in that country.

7. In America, earthball was a game of _____ during the New Games Tournament in Fort Cronkite, California.

8. The Japanese believed the team that was _____ in the game was assured of having a good crop in the next harvest.

Name: _____

Using New Words

mimicry	— the act of imitating closely
calculate	— to design or adapt for a purpose
creativity	— the quality of being creative
agile	— able to move quickly and easily
obstacle	— something that blocks or stands in the way
defy	— to boldly resist
guidance	— leadership, supervision
perceive	— to be aware of through the senses

Directions: Study the vocabulary words and their meanings. Then complete each sentence.

1. Follow the leader is a game that is based on imitation and _____ .

2. The fun of the game depends on the _____ of the leader as he or she presents new ideas to the followers.

3. Followers in the game must be _____ so that they can follow the leader.

4. Followers must accurately _____ the leader's motions each time he changes them.

5. The leader offers the only _____ that others see during the game.

6. If a follower _____ the leader, he or she is out of the game.

7. The leader tries to challenge the followers by using many _____ .

8. The leader must carefully _____ each move that he makes.

Using New Words

congregate	— gather
relay	— a crew, group or team that relieves another in a race
cherish	— to feel affection for
hilarious	— full of merriment
boundary	— a line or limit where something comes to the end
escalate	— to increase
spectator	— a person who watches an event
victorious	— to defeat an opponent

Directions: Study the vocabulary words and their meanings.
Use them to complete the story about Pickaback Races.

Pickaback Races

Pickaback races are often a favorite game among people who _____

for parties or picnics. Youngsters _____ the pickaback ride, but nearly

everyone loves a good race.

The game turns into a _____ event when older children and

grown-ups participate. It is as much fun for _____ as it is for the

participants, as people climb onto each other's backs and then slide off again.

During pickaback _____ , adults carry children or other adults on their backs.

They run to a _____ where the riders try to climb onto other adults'

backs without falling. Then the racers quickly run to another boundary. Those who run fastest

are usually _____. Everyone wants to win!

The fun _____ until the end of the race. By that time, participants

and spectators are sometimes laughing so hard it is hard for them to stand up, much less run!

Using New Words

vigorous	— full of energy, lively
rival	— competitor
primary	— first or foremost
technique	— a method by which a task is carried out
devise	— to think of, plan or invent
characteristically	— having the usual qualities
catapult	— to throw
function	— purpose or use

Directions: Study the vocabulary words and their meanings. Then complete each sentence in the story about hoop games.

Hoop Games

Hoops have been around for thousands of years. Ancient Greek doctors recommended that people use hula-hoops for _____ exercise.

Target shooting was the _____ reason that American Indian boys used hoops. They covered them with animal skins or woven fabric. Two lines of Indian boys faced each other and rolled the hoops back and forth. Players _____ darts at the rolling targets.

Some Eskimos used a similar _____ when playing hoop games, but they didn't cover their hoops. They rolled a hoop between two _____ and threw long poles through the big hole.

Hoops have had different _____ through the years. Children in Europe liked to bowl, or roll, hoops for fun. They bowled hoops by flinging them forward and running along beside them while pushing them with sticks or the palms of their hands.

Children who play with hula-hoops still _____ new uses for them. Today people _____ put hula-hoops around their waists and wriggle their bodies to spin them in circles. Doing the hula-hoop is good exercise.

Name: _____

Using New Words

superior	— of higher quality
bore	— to pierce
boredom	— the state of being uninterested
conquest	— the act of overcoming something
unconventional	— not following accepted practices, customs or tastes
deface	— to ruin the surface
duration	— the amount of time that something exists or occurs
covet	— to long for

Directions: Study the vocabulary words and their meanings. Then use them to complete the story about a game called Conkers.

Conkers: The Game of the Battling Chestnuts

Conkers is an _____ contest of conquering usually played with a chestnut tied to the end of a thick string. The object of the game is for one of the two battling chestnuts to crack or break.

English conker players believe that the best chestnuts for the game are found at the top of horse chestnut trees. They _____ those chestnuts!

Sometimes they use nuts that aren't as good, but they try to make them _____ by baking them or soaking them in salt water or vinegar. Children in some countries use walnuts or shells instead of chestnuts.

Players _____ a hole through the center of each chestnut with a screw or a nail so that it will easily slide onto the thick string.

Once a conker is made, one person challenges the other. Players take turns trying to crack or_____ each other's conker for the _____ of the battle. Once the _____ is completed, the game of conkers has ended. Conkers is certainly a way to eliminate_____.

Name: _____

Using New Words

follies	— foolish acts or ideas
ban	— to forbid by law
dispatch	— to send off quickly
pursue	— to chase in order to catch
essential	— very important, vital
gratify	— to give pleasure or satisfaction to
attain	— to achieve
hinder	— to make difficult

Directions: Study the vocabulary words and their meanings. Then use them to complete the story about the game of chase. You will need to add "**ed**" or "**es**" to some of the words.

Prisoner's Base is a Game of Chase

At one time or another, nearly every child has been _____ by a hearty game of chase. But rarely do adults participate. That wasn't the case, though, many years ago when King Edward III had to _____ a game called Prisoner's Base from Westminster Palace. So many adults were playing it that it _____ the governing of the land.

Plenty of outdoor open space is _____ for Prisoner's Base, which is played in a large, square area. The space is equally divided in two. Each team has a "home" and a "prison" in its half of the square. Team members occupy their homes, which are in opposite corners.

A circle is drawn in the middle of the line that divides the two teams. The captain of one team _____ a runner to the circle. The other team captain sends a runner to _____ him or her. The first team's captain then sends a second person into the chase. The object of the game is to get the runners from the opposite team into "prison."

Prisoner's Base is fun. But often the game is full of _____ because people argue or disagree about the rules. Usually the game ends before the goal can be _____ .

Using New Words

joust	— to compete
competitors	— opponents
rap	— to strike quickly and sharply
circumstances	— a condition, fact or event that is related to and may affect something else
clasp	— a strong grasp or hold
cordial	— friendly
ruthless	— showing no pity
taunt	— to say or do mean things

Directions: Study the vocabulary words and their meanings. Then complete the story about egg jousting, an old form of entertainment.

Egg Games

In parts of Russia each spring children use red eggs to _____ with each other. Two children, each holding an egg, battle it out by trying to break their opponent's egg shell. Egg jousters are not _____ to each other. They sometimes _____ and tease each other during a jousting match.

When egg jousting, the pointed end of the egg is called the "head" and the rounded end is called the "heel." The challenger often says something like, "With my head I will break your head." The _____ sometimes calls for a jouster to brag that he will win the battle. A _____ battle follows. Each child holds his egg and positions it to protect it from the other.

Players _____ each other's eggs, trying to crack them. Each protects his egg by _____ it tightly with his hand, so that little of the egg can be seen or hit.

Once an egg has been broken on both its head and its heel, the player must use another egg to stay in the game. The winner is the player who has eggs left at the end of the game.

Name: _____

Review

superior	— of higher quality
pursue	— to chase in order to catch
opponents	— competitors
duration	— the amount of time that something exists or occurs
boundary	— a line or limit where something comes to an end
cherish	— to feel affection for
agile	— able to move quickly and easily
victor	— one who defeats an opponent

Directions: Study the vocabulary words and their meanings. Then use them to complete the story about Indian Kickball.

Indian Kickball

Kickball is played by the Hopi Indians of the Southwestern United States. In this game, _____ kick a ball for the length of a course, which is at least a mile long.

Two teams, with an equal number of three to six people on each, _____ balls from one _____ to another. Team members must be quick and _____ to participate in the sport.

The Hopi Indians and the Tarahumara Indians of Mexico _____ Indian kickball. There is much festivity throughout the _____ of each game.

Most Native Americans play kickball with their bare right feet. They practice lifting the ball with their toes and throwing it forward. Indian kickball requires a lot of team work. No one tries to dominate the ball the whole time.

Each team attempts to beat its opponent to the boundary at the other end of the field. The winning team is considered _____ . It is the _____ , at least until the next game.

Name: _____

Locating Information

The table of contents, located in the front of books or magazines, tells a lot about what's inside.

Tables of contents in books list the headings and page numbers for each chapter. Chapters are the parts into which books are divided. Also listed are chapter numbers, the sections and subsections, if any. Look at the sample table of contents below:

Contents:	
1. Planting a garden	2
Location	4
Fences	5
2. Seeds	8
Vegetables	
Potatoes	9
Beans	10
Tomatoes	11
Fruit	
Melons	13
Pumpkins	14
3. Caring for a garden	15
Weeding	16
Fertilizing	19

Directions: After reading about the table of contents, follow these instructions. Answer the questions about the book.

1. How many chapters are in this book? _____

2. What chapter contains information about things to plant? _____

3. On what page does information about fences begin? _____

4. What chapter tells you what you can use to help your garden grow better? _____

5. What page tells you how to use fertilizer? _____

6. What page tells you how far apart to plant pumpkin seeds? _____

7. What is on page 11? _____

8. What is on page 4? _____

Name: _____

Locating Information

Directions: The table of contents below is divided into units and sections. Units are parts into which a book is divided. Sections are segments of each unit.

Table of Contents

UNIT ONE: The Sun	1	**UNIT THREE:** Constellations	65
A Bright Light	5	Big Dipper	67
A Hot Star	10	Little Dipper	69
		Polaris	71
UNIT TWO: The Planets	12	Others	74
Mercury	15		
Venus	21	**UNIT FOUR:** Space Wonders	98
Earth	27	Comets	101
Mars	32	Meteors and Meteorites	105
Jupiter	39		
Saturn	49		
Neptune	58		
Pluto	61		

1. How many units are in this book? _____
2. Where would you find information about life on Mars? _____
3. Where would you find information about the sun's heat and brightness? _____
4. What is on page 27?

5. The Milky Way is a group of stars, or a constellation. Where would you find information about it? _____
6. What is on page 101?

7. Where would you get information about the moons that orbit Jupiter? _____

8. How many pages about Earth are in this book? _____

9. How many pages in this book are about Polaris? _____

10. Where would you find out about the Big Dipper? _____

Name: _____

Locating Information

In some magazines, tables of contents list articles in numerical order. The soccer article begins on page 5, the baseball article begins on page 7, the football story begins on page 13, and so on.

Other magazines' tables of contents are organized by subjects, by columns and by features. Subjects are the topics covered in the articles. A feature is a specific kind of article, such as an article about sports or about cooking. "Feature" also has another meaning. A "regular feature" is something that appears in every issue, such as letters to the editor, movie reviews, sports statistics and other things. Some magazines also call regular features "departments."

Columns are another kind of "regular feature" published in every issue. Columns are often written by the same person each time. A person who writes columns is called a columnist!

Most magazines' tables of contents will also give you an idea of what a story is about. Look at the sample below.

Kids' Life

Articles
- 8 Skateboarding in the U.S.A.
     Read about kids from across the country
     and how they make the best of their boards!
- 12 Summer Camp
      Believe it or not, camp is fun!
- 20 Battle of Gettysburg
      It was a decisive one in the American Civil War.
- 25 Snacks in a Flash
      Look at these treats you can make yourself!
- 29 Martin Luther King
      The man who made people think twice.

Comics
- 6 Little People
- 14 Skatin' Sam
- 30 Double Trouble

Columns
- 7 Videos
- 32 The Great Outdoors
- 39 The Fun and Famous

Departments
- 34 Your Health
- 36 Sports
- 38 Letters to the Editor

Directions: After reading about tables of contents in magazines, answer these questions about *Kids' Life* magazine.

1. What page does the story about summer camp begin on? _____

2. What page does the sports department begin on? _____

3. List the titles of the departments in this magazine:

1) _____ 2) _____ 3) _____

4. Can you tell what the Battle of Gettysburg was by reading the table of contents? _____
   What was it? _____

5. Is there any information in this magazine about roller skating?

_____

Name: _____

Locating Information

LIVING

Table of Contents

EXERCISE Ride for a while with these experienced cyclists. 13

DISCOVERIES Walk with a man through the ditches where he discovered dinosaur bones. 27

HAPPENINGS Earth Day becomes important once again. 5

SCIENCE Find out why astronauts like their jobs. 45

MUSIC Tunes that they sing in the mountains. 33

PEOPLE Read about Dan Quayle and how he got to be Vice President. 20
Talk to Jim Henson, the man behind the Muppets™. 28

SPORTS Why the Cleveland Indians won't win the title. 42

HISTORY A look at the lives of soldiers who were at Valley Forge. 39

DEPARTMENTS

Living Well 6   Letters to the Editor 9
Comedy 12   Books 16
Movies 24   Snacks 36

Directions: Look at the table of contents above for *Living* magazine. The articles in it are grouped according to subjects.

1. How many departments are in this issue of the magazine? _____

2. Circle the topics that are regular features in "*Living.*"

Books	Dinosaurs	Cleveland Indians	Dan Quayle
Comedy	Living Well	Snacks	Earth Day

3. Is this table of contents arranged alphabetically, in the order that articles appear, or by subjects? _____

4. What page would you look at if you wanted to see what was playing at movie theaters? _____

5. Is there any information in this magazine about football? _____

6. Who are the two people featured in this issue?

_____

7. Is there anything in this issue about cycling? _____

8. Under what heading is it listed? _____

Locating Information

An index is an alphabetical listing of names, topics and important words found in the back of a book. An index lists every page on which these items appear. For example, in a book about music, dulcimer might be listed this way: dulcimer 2, 13, 26, 38. Page numbers may also be listed like this: guitars 18-21. That means that information about guitars begins on page 18 and continues through page 21. Other words to know about indexes include:

subject — the name of the item in an index

sub-entry — a smaller division of the subject. For example, "apples" would be listed under "fruit."

N
Neptune, ...27
NGC 5128 (galaxy), ...39
Novas, ...32

O
Observatories. *See* El Caracol
Orbits of planets, ...10
Orion rocket, ...43

P
Planetoids. *See* Asteroids.
Planet rings
Jupiter, ...23
Saturn, ...9, 25
Uranus, ...26
Planets
discovered by Greeks, ...7
outside the solar system, ...40
visible with naked eye, ...9

See also planet names.
Pleiades, ...32
Pluto, ...12, 27
Polaris, ...35, 36
Pole star. *See* Polaris.
Project Ozma, ...41

R
Rings. *See* Planet rings.

S
Sagittarius, ...37
Satellites
Jupiter, ...24
Neptune, ...27
Pluto, ...27
Saturn, ...25
Uranus, ...26
See also Galilean satellites
Saturn, ...25

Directions: Look at part of the index from a book about the solar system. Then answer the questions.

1. On what pages is there information about Pluto? _____

2. On what page is information about Saturn's ring first found? _____

3. What is on page 41? _____

4. Where is there information about the pole star? _____

5. What is on page 43? _____

6. On what page would you find information about planets that are visible to the eye? _____

7. On what page would you find information about Jupiter's satellites? _____

Name: _____

Locating Information

Look at the index from a book about music. The letters A, B, C, D, E, F and G after some of the page numbers refer to the names of the units in which the pages are located. Each unit starts with page number one.

Unit A is Listening to Music.

Unit C is Instruments and Orchestras.

Unit E is The Story of Music.

Unit G is Writing Music.

Unit B is Music Around the World.

Unit D is Singing and Dancing.

Unit F is Composers and Their Music.

Index

b

Bach, C.P.E. F3
Bach, J.C. F3
Bach, J.S. A14, B28, D6, E19, F2-3, F7, G12, G13
backing A12, C27
background music B5, see incidental music
bagpipes B30-1
ballad E21
Ballade A12, F8
ballet D26-32, E30
bands B13, B22-3, B30-2
baritone (brass instrument) C10
baritone voice D7
Baroque music D10, D18, D20, E16-17
Bartok F4, F24
bass voice D4, D7
bassoon B31, C4, C6, C24

beating time C29
Beatles A15, A25, B28, C27
Bedford F32
Beethoven A16, B6, B14, E20, E24, F5, F7, F11, G3, G8-9, G13-14
Berlioz E24, F6
Bizet D12
Borodin F24
Brahms A12, A16, E26, F17, F25, G13
brass bands B32
brass instruments B23, C7-10, C24
Britten A9, D12, F28, G13
Bronze Age E5
bugle C10
buskers B17
Byrd E12

Directions: Answer the questions about the index.

1. On what page is there information about beating time? _____

2. What subject is mentioned on pages A15, A25, B28 and C27? _____

3. On what page is there information about brass bands? _____

4. What other entry includes the word "brass?" _____

5. Where else is there information about background music? _____

6. On what page is there information about bugles? _____

7. List all pages that mention Beethoven. _____

8. What instrument is discussed on pages B30 and B31? _____

Name: _____

Locating Information

APPETIZERS
Bacon-wrapped Halibut..92
Scallops with Sorrel and Tomato 116
Shrimp and Basil Beignets...116
Shrimp and Vegetable Spring Rolls with Hoisin and Mustard Sauces 85
Sweet Potato Ribbon Chips 136

SOUPS
Lemongrass Soup, Hot, with Radishes and Chives 84
Roasted Garlic Soup 22
Vegetable Soup with Creamy Asparagus Flan 154

SALADS, SALAD DRESSINGS
Arugula Salad with Roasted Beets, Walnuts and Daikon 158
Chicken, Fennel, Orange and Olive Salad 24
Jicama Salad 81
Tomato, Onion and Zucchini Salad 152
Walnut Vinaigrette 158

Directions: Some magazines are beginning to use simple indexes to guide their readers to information that they contain. Look at the segment of an index in *Bon Appetit* magazine. Then answer the questions.

1. How many kinds of salads are listed in this issue? _____

2. What is the recipe that contains radishes? _____

3. Name the recipe found on page 24. _____

4. On what page would you find an appetizer that includes scallops? _____

   What is the name of this recipe? _____

5. Can you find any listings that contain halibut, _____
   a kind of fish?

6. On what page is there a recipe made from sweet potatoes? _____

   What is the name of the recipe? _____

   For what part of a meal would it be served? _____

Name: _____

Review

FARMING

Table of Contents

9   *Farmers of the Midwest*
    Read about small
    farmers still
    trying to survive in
    the business.

15 *Farmers' Markets*
    Some farmers take
    their goods to town
    and sell them to the
    city folk.

26 *Hay: The Cheapest Way*
    New technology helps
    produce bales of hay
    quicker and cheaper than
    in the past.

36 *The Farm Family*
    Farming is a way of
    life and everybody helps!

Departments

Letters to the Editor 5
Finances 7
High Tech 13
Haymaker 27

INDEX

Africa 6
Alabama 49
Alps 21, 25
Antarctica 10-12
Antarctic Circle 8-10
Arctic 12-14
Arctic Circle 14
Arctic Ocean 15
Asia 37
Athens 33
Atlantic Ocean 11

Baltic Sea 15, 30
Baltimore 51
Black Sea 37
Bombay 39
Brazil 59
British Isles 19
Buffalo 52
Bug River 31

Cadiz 27
California 48
Cambridge 19
Cape of Good Hope 49
China 11, 41
Colorado River, Argentina 61
Colorado River, U.S.A. 62
Continents 2-3
Cuba 55

Directions: Look at the table of contents from "*Farming*" magazine. Then answer the questions.

1. Is there any information about fashion in
   this magazine? _____

2. Is there any information about computers? _____

3. Information about children on farms is probably
   included in which feature? _____

4. Are there any features about animals
   in this magazine? _____

Now look at the index from a book about the world. Then answer the questions.

1. On what pages would you find information
   about the Baltic Sea? _____

2. What is listed on pages 2-3?

_____

3. Where are the two Colorado Rivers? _____

Using Newspapers For Research

Newspapers are publications regularly printed and distributed, usually daily or weekly, containing news, opinions, advertisements and other information of general interest.

Newspaper indexes are reference sources you can use to find which newspapers printed articles on a variety of topics. The indexes also tell the publication dates and page numbers of the articles. Some libraries have indexes of their local newspapers on file cards. Large newspapers, such as the *Washington Post* and the *New York Times*, have printed indexes that they sell to libraries.

The *National Newspaper Index* is a listing of topics from five large newspapers: *The New York Times, The Christian Science Monitor*, the *Wall Street Journal*, the *Los Angeles Times,* and the *Washington Post*. The *National Newspaper Index* lists articles that have appeared within the last three years, according to their subjects. Some libraries have the *National Newspaper Index* on microfilm. Others have it on a data base. Printed indexes for newspapers included in the *National Newspaper Index* are also available at many libraries.

Most local libraries keep old editions of newspapers on microfilm. Microfilm is a photograph of printed material that is reduced in size and put on film. Strips of microfilm are much easier to store than printed versions of newspapers.

Directions: Answer these questions about newspapers and their indexes.

1. Newspapers contain information on

_____ .

2. The key to finding information in a newspaper is using the _____ .

3. The _____ and the _____
have printed indexes.

4. The _____ lists articles from five large newspapers.

5. The five newspapers included in the *National Newspaper Index* are

_____

_____

6. Articles from the last _____ years are listed in the *National Newspaper Index*.

7. The *National Newspaper Index*, which combines topics from all five newspapers, is

available on _____ or on_____ .

Using Newspapers For Research

News digests are books that contain summaries of news events. They are produced by clipping services that use articles from many newspapers. They are then compiled into one book or microfilm listing. News digests provide libraries with information from newspapers that they do not receive. There are different kinds of news digests. Listed below are two that provide only American news.

1. *Editorials on File* includes introductions to current news topics, followed by 15 or 20 editorials from United States and Canadian newspapers. It is produced twice a month.

2. *NewsBank* reproduces articles from nearly 200 American newspapers. It is produced on microfiche four times a year. Microfiche is a sheet of microfilm containing rows of printed pages that have been reduced in size. *NewsBank* has a printed index listing subjects and names that are included in articles.

Here are three digests that provide news from around the world.

1. *Facts on File: World News Digest with Index* (FOF) summarizes major events each week from throughout the world.

2. *ISLA: Information Services on Latin America* reprints articles about Central America each month from seven large American newspapers and two British newspapers.

3. *Keesing's Contemporary Archives: Record of World Events* analyzes political and economic events each week that have happened around the world.

Directions: In which news digest described above would you would find the following information?

1. An editorial about a current event? _____

2. Articles from American newspapers on microfiche. _____

3. An article analyzing an election in South America.

_____

4. A summary of an international sports event. _____

5. Editorials from several American newspapers that talk about the U.S. presidential election.

_____

6. An article about the country of Guatemala, located in Central America.

_____

Name: _____

Using Newspapers For Research

Some news digests contain information from foreign newspapers that have been translated into English. These digests provide information about events in other countries.

1. *African Recorder: a Fortnightly Record of African Events* includes articles from African and Asian newspapers, magazines, radio broadcasts and government sources published each week.

2. *Asian Recorder: Weekly Digest of Asian Events* is similar to the *African Recorder* and gathers much of its news from the same sources each week.

3. *Canadian News Facts: The Indexed Digest of Canadian Current Events (CNF)* summarizes articles from 20 leading Canadian newspapers and several news agencies. It is published every two weeks.

4. *Current Digest of the Soviet Press (CDSP)* translates some articles from Soviet magazines and newspapers (such as Pravda) into the English language each week.

5. *Foreign Broadcast Information Service (FBIS)* reports news each day about China, Central America, Eastern Europe and the Soviet Union taken from television broadcasts, newspapers, press agencies and governement statements.

Directions: Answer these questions about how to get information from other countries.

1. The _____ and the _____ gather
   news from African and Asian newspapers, magazines, radio broadcasts and government
   sources.

2. Translations of Russian articles can be found in the _____.

3. The *Foreign Broadcast Information Service* reprints news from sources in

_____ and _____ .

4. Summaries of articles taken from 20 Canadian newspapers are included in

_____ .

5. Articles from *Pravda* can be found in _____.

6. The only daily report listed above is the _____ .

7. Summaries of articles about Canada's schools can be found in

_____ .

Name: _____

Using Newspapers For Research

Articles from old newspapers are on file in some libraries. The *Great Contemporary Issues Series* is a group of books that contains articles. Some reprinted from the *New York Times* are from as far back as the 1860s. More than 30 books are in the series, ranging in topics from big business to China to medicine to health care. Here are the names of other collections of newspapers that also can be found in some local libraries.

1. *Canadian Newspapers on Microfilm* has more than 300 Canadian newspapers from the 1800s and 1900s.

2. *Civil War Newspapers on Microfilm* includes more than 300 articles from newspapers printed during the Civil War, from 1861 to 1865.

3. *Contemporary Newspapers of the North American Indian* includes 49 newspapers from several states during 1960s and 1970s.

4. *Early American Newspapers* includes copies of some of the newspapers listed in the book *History and Bibliography of American Newspapers, 1690-1820.*

5. *Negro Newspapers on Microfilm* includes parts and entire copies of nearly 200 black American newspapers published from the mid-1800s to the mid-1900s.

6. *The Newspapers of Ireland* includes 25 newspapers from that country published in the 1800s and early 1900s.

Directions: Answer these questions about old newspapers.

1. Newspapers from the Civil War era can be found in

_____ .

2. *Early American Newspapers* contains copies of papers published from
_____ to _____ .

3. Old newspapers from Ireland can be found in _____ .

4. Copies of newspapers that are listed in *History and Bibliography of American Newspapers, 1690-1820* can be found in_____ .

5. One of the best places to find information about slavery during the American Civil War would be _____ .

6. Information about Indians in 1971 could be found by looking in the _____

_____ .

7. Information about early elections in Canada could be found in _____

_____ .

Name: _____

Using Newspapers For Research

When libraries borrow books, magazines or newspapers from other libraries it is called interlibrary loan. To find out which libraries have certain newspapers, use one of these two sources: *Newspapers in Microform: U.S., 1948-72* or *Newspapers in Microform: Foreign Countries, 1948-72.*

The *American Library Directory* provides addresses of libraries throughout the country. Look at this listing from the *American Library Directory.* All of these libraries are in Massachusetts. Their towns are listed in bold at the top of each entry.

CLARKSBURG — 1871. Area code 413

P   NORTH ADAMS PUBLIC LIBRARY, Church St, North Adams, 01247. SAN 307-3327. Tel 413-662-2545. *Librn* Lisa Jarisch Founded 1884. Pop served 16,000; Circ 60,000
1988-89 Income $163,444. Exp $28,415, Bks $23,500, Per $3500, Other Print Mat $65, Micro $225, AV Mats $1125; Sal $111,000
Library Holdings: Bk vols 40,000; Per sub 120
Mem of Western Regional Pub Libr Syst

CLINTON — 12,771. Area code 508

P   BIGELOW FREE PUBLIC LIBRARY, 54 Walnut St, 01510. SAN 307-3335. Tel 508-365-5052; Interlibrary Loan Service Tel. No.: 799-1683. *Librn* Christine Flaherty
Pop served 12,891; Circ 40,981
1987-88 Income $104,330. Exp Bks $18,600, Per $3000, AV Mats $500; Sal $74,182
Library Holdings: Bk vols 105,000
Mem of Cent Mass Regional Libr Syst

COLRAIN — 1552. Area code 413

P   GRISWOLD MEMORIAL LIBRARY, Main St, 01340. SAN 307-
Founded 1908. Pop served 1493

Directions: Use the information above to answer the following questions.

1. What is it called when libraries borrow newspapers and other materials from other libraries? _____

2. To find a newspaper printed in the United States in 1968, where would you look?

_____

3. How would you locate a German newspaper from 1950?

_____

4. Addresses for libraries throughout the country can be found in what publication?

_____

5. In the listing from the *American Library Directory,* "Lbrn" is the abbreviation for librarian. Who is the librarian at the North Adams Public Library?_____

Name: _____

Using Newspapers For Research

Although some newspapers are no longer published, libraries still may have information about them. The *History and Bibliography of American Newspapers, 1690-1820,* is a reference book that documents newspapers from throughout those years. Another book, *American Newspapers, 1821-1936,* lists more newspapers. Newspapers that are published today are listed in the *Gale Directory of Publications and Broadcast Medias.*

Look at this listing for the *Tule River Times* taken from the *Gale Directory.* The number, 3695, is the listing number for that newspaper.

SPRINGVILLE
Print

3695 Tule River Times
P.O. Box 692
Springville, CA 93265   Phone: (209) 539-3166
Community newspaper. **Estab.:** August 1979. **Frequency:** Weekly.
Printing Method: Offset. **Trim Size:** 11 1/4x14. Cols./Page: 5.
Col Width: 11 picas.   **Col. Depth:** 13 in. **Key Personnel:** Pamela Holve,
Managing Editor and Co-Publisher.
Subscription: $15.00.
Ad Rate: BW: $185.25   **Circulation:** Paid +1,000
         PCI: $3.15   Free +12
Color advertising not accepted.

Directions: Answer these questions about newspaper directories.

1. What publication would list newspapers printed in 1790?
_____

2. Where would a newspaper printed in 1889 be listed?
_____

3. To find newspapers published in California today, where would you look?
_____

4. How often is the *Tule River Times* published? _____

5. Does the *Gale Directory* list the page size of the *Tule River Times*? (Tip: Look for the words "Trim Size.")
_____

6. When was the *Tule River Times* established? _____

7. What is the telephone number of the *Tule River Times*? _____

8. What is the cost of a subscription to the *Tule River Times*? _____

Name: _____

Using Newspapers For Research

Directions: Choose one of the newspaper projects listed below and complete it at your local library. Use this page for notes.

1. Use the *National Newspaper Index* to find articles about ice hockey player Wayne Gretzky. On a separate piece of paper, list five of these articles and the newspapers in which they appeared. Find one of the articles in the microfilm files at the library. Summarize the article after you have read it.

2. Use *Editorials on File* at the library to find 10 of the current editorial topics addressed by newspapers. List the topics on a separate sheet of paper. Do any of them address education or health issues? Read several editorial summaries on those or other subjects in the booklet and write a brief report about them.

3. Use *Facts on File: World News Digest with Index* to find summaries of any articles related to the space exploration program in the Soviet Union. Write a brief report about these summaries.

4. Use the latest issue of the *Current Digest of the Soviet Press* to find articles about Russian teenagers. Use that information to write a story about them.

_____
_____
_____
_____
_____
_____
_____
_____
_____
_____
_____
_____
_____
_____
_____
_____

Name: _____

Review

Directions: Read each question. Then choose one of the news digests listed in the box to answer it.

> **News Digests:**
> The New York Times Index
> The National Newspaper Index
> Editorials on File
> NewsBank
> African Recorder
> Asian Recorder
> ISLA: Information Services on Latin America
> Current Digest of the Soviet Press
> Foreign Broadcast Information Service
> Great Contemporary Issue Series
> Civil War Newspapers on Microfilm
> Contemporary Newspapers of the North American Indian
> Early American Newspapers, 1704-1820
> Negro Newspapers on Microfilm
> Newspapers in Microform: U.S.
> Newspapers in Microform: Foreign Countries
> Gale Directory

1. Which publication includes American newspapers published from 1704-1820?

_____

2. Where are newspapers of today listed?

_____

3. Which publication includes summaries of editorials written in several newspapers?

_____

4. Where would articles about Soviet school reform be found?

_____

5. Name the series of books that includes articles from the *New York Times* dating back to 1860?

_____

6. Where would an article about slavery in the mid-1800s be reproduced?

_____

7. Name five publications that include articles from foreign newspapers:

　1) _____   2) _____

　3) _____   4) _____

　5) _____

Name: _____

Doing Biographical Research

A biography is a written history of a person's life. Often information for a biography can be obtained from an encyclopedia, especially if a person is famous. Of course, not everyone is listed in a main article in an encyclopedia. Use the encyclopedia's index, which is the last book in the set, to find which volume contains the information you need. Look at this listing taken from an encyclopedia index for Henry Moore, an English artist:

MOORE, HENRY English sculptor, 1898-1986
    main article Moore 12:106b, illus.
    references in Sculpture 15:290a, illus.

LINCOLN, ABRAHAM president of US, 1809-65
    main article Lincoln 11:49a, illus.
    references in
        Assassination 2:64b
        Caricature: illus. 4:87
        Civil War, American 4:296a fol.
        Confederate States of America 5:113b fol.
        Democracy 6:17a
        Gettysburg, Battle of 8:144a
        Illinois 9:259b
        Thanksgiving Day 17:199a
        United States of America, history of 18:137a fol.
        Westward Movement 19:49a
LINCOLN, BENJAMIN US army officer, 1733-1810
    references in American Revolution 1:204b
LIND, JENNY Swedish singer, 1820-87;

operatic soprano admired for vocal purity and control; made debut 1838 in Stockholm and sang in Paris and London becoming known as the "Swedish Nightingale"; toured US with P.T. Barnum 1850; last concert 1883
    references in Barnum 2:235a
LINDBERGH, ANNE US aviator, b. 1907
    references in Lindbergh 11:53b, illus.
LINDBERGH, CHARLES AUGUSTUS US aviator, 1902-74
    main article Lindbergh 11:53a, illus.
    references in
        Aviation, history of 2:140b, illus.
        Medals and decorations 11:266b
        Saint Louis 15:215b
LINDE, KARL VON German engineer, 1842-1934
    references in Refrigeration 15:32b

Notice that the listing includes Henry Moore's dates of birth and death. It also includes a short description of his accomplishments: he was an English sculptor. Look below at part of the index from the *Children's Britannica* encyclopedias. Then answer the questions.

Directions: Answer these questions about biographical research.

1. Where is the main article for Abraham Lincoln?

_____

2. In addition to the main article, how many other places are there references to Abraham Lincoln? _____

3. In which encyclopedia volume is there information about Anne Lindbergh? _____

4. What is the title of the main article in which Anne Lindbergh is mentioned? _____

Name: _____

Doing Biographical Research

If a person has been in the news recently, check the *National Newspaper Index* or an index for the local newspaper to find articles. The *National Newspaper Index* contains the names of articles published by five major newspapers within the last three years. *NewsBank*, a news digest containing information from nearly 200 newspapers throughout the country, should also be checked.

Also check the *Obituary Index to the New York Times* or the *Obituary Index to the (London, England) Times*. Obituaries are notices of deaths. They usually include a brief biography of the person.

Reader's Guide to Periodical Literature alphabetically lists subjects of articles printed in most major magazines. A *Reader's Guide* entry lists the magazine in which an article appeared, the date of the publication and the page number where the article starts.

Biography Index lists biographical articles published since 1946.

Almanacs also contain information about individuals. For example, *The Kid's World Almanac of Records and Facts* lists the United States presidents and their major accomplishments. It also has information about athletes, composers and others.

Directions: Use encyclopedias and one or more of the resources listed above to research one of the following people. Begin writing your biographical report in the space provided. (If you need more room, use a separate sheet of paper.)

Research topics:

Richard M. Nixon	Jesse Jackson
Mother Teresa	Lech Walesa
Margaret Thatcher	Mikhail Gorbachev

_____

_____

_____

_____

_____

_____

_____

_____

Name: _____

Doing Biographical Research

Biographical dictionaries, such as *Who's Who*, contain histories of peoples' lives. In addition to *Who's Who*, there are many other biographical dictionaries. BDs, as they are called, can include books such as the *Biographical Dictionary of English Architects* or *Who's Who in Art Materials*. Some biographical dictionaries list only people who lived during certain eras, such as *Women Artists: 1550-1950*.

Because there are so many biographical dictionaries, master indexes are published to guide researchers. Up to 500 books are listed in some biographical master indexes. A master index may list several biographical dictionaries in which information about a person can be obtained.

There are several different biographical master indexes. Here are a few.

1. The *Biography and Genealogy Master Index* contains 11 books and is a good place to begin research. Parts of this index, such as *Children's Authors and Illustrators*, are in separate volumes.

2. *An Analytical Bibliography of Universal Collected Biography* contains information from more than 3,000 biographical dictionaries published before 1933.

3. *In Black and White: A Guide to Magazine Articles, Newspaper Articles and Books Concerning More than 15,000 Black Individuals and Groups* is the title of a large biographical master index.

4. *Marquis Who's Who Publications: Index to All Books* lists names from at least 15 *Who's Who* books published by Marquis each year.

Directions: Complete each sentence about biographical master indexes.

1. Biographical dictionaries contain

_____

2. When beginning research in biographical dictionaries, first use a

_____

3. The __ has 11 books in its set.

_____

4. *Children's Authors and Illustrators* is a separate volume of the

_____

5. Information from at least 15 *Who's Who* publications each year is contained in the

_____

6. Information from old biographical dictionaries can be found in

_____

Doing Biographical Research

Directions: Use biographical dictionaries to research a person listed below. Remember to begin with one or more biographical master indexes. There may be more than one biographical dictionary that contains information about the person. Write a report about that person's life in the space provided. Use additional paper, if necessary.

Ronald Reagan	Woody Allen	Elizabeth Dole
John Glenn	Andrew Lloyd Webber	Elizabeth Taylor

_____

_____

_____

_____

_____

_____

_____

_____

_____

_____

_____

_____

_____

_____

_____

Name: _____

Doing Biographical Research

There are several ways to find if a person has written any books or articles. The *National Union Catalog* is the published card catalog of the Library of Congress. It is considered the best resource for finding names of authors.

Researchers also use *Books in Print*, which lists books published from 1948 through today. The author volume of *Books in Print* is used to research a person. The *Cumulative Book Index: a World List of Books in the English Language* lists books published from 1898 through today.

If the person being researched has written a book, critics' reviews will give public reaction to the book. Periodical indexes, such as *Reader's Guide to Periodical Literature,* alphabetically lists authors of articles in its index.

The *Biography Index, 1876-1949* and the *Biography Index, 1950 to 1980* lists biographical articles about a person. *Biographical Books* lists books written about people from 1876 to 1980.

The *Subject Guide to Books in Print* contains titles of biographies published from 1957 through today. The *Library of Congress Dictionary Catalog: Subjects* contains names of books published from 1950 through today. Both of these books contain the same information available in *Biographical Books*.

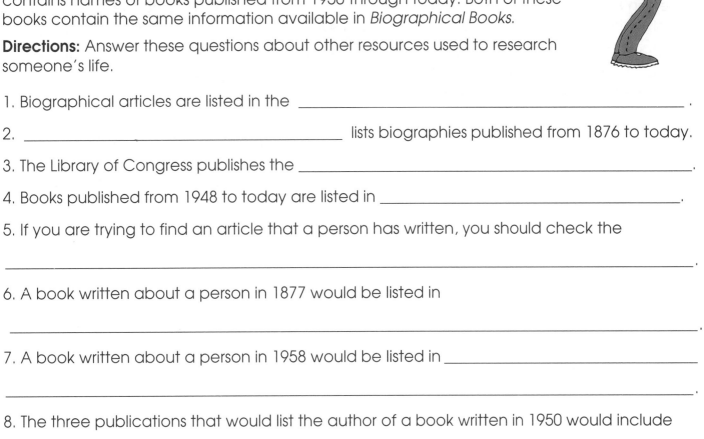

Directions: Answer these questions about other resources used to research someone's life.

1. Biographical articles are listed in the _____ .

2. _____ lists biographies published from 1876 to today.

3. The Library of Congress publishes the _____ .

4. Books published from 1948 to today are listed in _____ .

5. If you are trying to find an article that a person has written, you should check the

_____ .

6. A book written about a person in 1877 would be listed in

_____ .

7. A book written about a person in 1958 would be listed in _____

_____ .

8. The three publications that would list the author of a book written in 1950 would include

_____ .

Name: _____

Doing Biographical Research

Information about people who belong to clubs, trade unions or other organizations can sometimes be found in libraries or from an organization's main office. If these people worked for corporations, information may be obtained by contacting the public relations office of that company.

Unpublished materials, such as diaries or letters, are usually donated to a library or a historical society when a person dies. Clues that such materials exist may be found when reading other books or articles about a person.

Personal interviews can also provide information about subjects. A few points to remember when conducting an interview:

1. Cover the five main points that you need to know for any story: who, what, when, where and why.
2. Write accurate notes while doing the interview.
3. Use the notes to write the article.
4. If your notes are unclear, check them with the person interviewed.
5. Double check other facts that you are not sure about. Be sure to check the spelling of the person's name and check important dates that were mentioned during the interview.
6. Only write things that you are sure the person said.

Directions: After reading about other ways to research a person's life, use the tips listed above to conduct an interview with a friend or classmate. Write a brief biography containing what you learned during the interview.

_____

_____

_____

_____

_____

_____

_____

_____

Name: _____

Doing Biographical Research

Directions: Look at the names listed below. Choose one of them to research, then write a biographical article on a separate sheet of paper. Put a check beside each listed resource you used. (You may not have to use all of them.)

Subjects:

Judy Blume, author
Dale Murphy, baseball player
Henry J. Heimlich, doctor
Diana Ross, singer
Ted Kennedy, politician

Check these sources:

_____ Encyclopedia

_____ Biographical Master Index

_____ Biographical Dictionary

_____ *National Union Catalog*

_____ *Books in Print*

_____ *Cumulative Book Index: a World List of Books in the English Language*

_____ Book Reviews

_____ *Reader's Guide to Periodical Index*

_____ *Biography Index*

_____ *Biographical Books, 1876-1949*

_____ *Biographical Books, 1950-1980*

_____ *Subject Guide to Books in Print*

_____ *Library of Congress Dictionary Catalog: Subjects*

_____ *National Newspaper Index*

_____ *Newsbank Personal Papers*

Name: _____

Review

Directions: Read each heading and follow the instructions.

A. Write **T** or **F** on the line beside each statement.

_____ 1. Do not use a biographical master index before checking *Who's Who in American Education.*

_____ 2. A biographical dictionary lists people and their histories.

_____ 3. The *Biographical Dictonary of English Architects* is a *Biographical Master Index.*

_____ 4. A biographical master index includes listings from only one biographical dictionary.

B. Choose the correct word from the word box to complete each sentence.

articles	index	contents	atlases	resource	almanacs

1. Before finding a listing in an encyclopedia, you should use the encyclopedia _____.

2. The *Reader's Guide to Periodical Literature* lists _____ published in most major magazines.

3. *Biography Index* is a _____ that lists articles published about people since 1946.

4. _____ list odd bits of information about people.

C. Write **book** or **article** on the line to tell whether the index named would list books or articles.

1. *Biography Index* _____

2. *Reader's Guide to Periodical Literature* _____

3. *Books in Print* _____

4. *National Union Catalog* _____

D. Fill in the blanks to complete the sentences.

1. A person's original writings would include his diary or _____ .

2. If a person worked for a corporation, you could gain information about him or her by contacting that firm's _____ office.

Determining The Author's Purpose

Authors write to entertain, inform or persuade. To entertain means to hold the attention of or to amuse someone. A fiction book about outerspace entertains its reader, as does a joke book.

To inform means to give factual information. A cookbook informs the reader of new recipes. A newspaper tells what is happening in the world.

To persuade means to convince. Newspaper editorial writers try to persuade readers to accept their opinions. Doctors write health columns to persuade readers to eat healthy foods.

Directions: Look at the passages below. Tell whether they entertain, inform or persuade. (They may do more than one.) Give the reasons why. The first one is done for you.

George Washington was born in a brick house near the Potomac River in Virginia on Feb. 11, 1732. When he was 11 years old, George went to live with his half-brother, Lawrence, at Mount Vernon.

Author's Purpose: _To Inform_

Reason: _It gives factual information_

When George Washington was a child, he always measured and counted things. Maybe that is why he became a surveyor when he grew up. Surveyors like to measure and count things, too.

Author's Purpose: _____

Reason: _____

George Washington was the best president Americans ever had. He led a new nation to Independence. He made all of the states feel as if they were part of the United States. All presidents should be as involved with the country as George Washington.

Author's Purpose: _____

Reason: _____

Before George Washington was married, he loved to dance with women at parties. He fell in love many times. Before he met his wife, Martha, he proposed to two other women. They both turned him down, but George Washington was not defeated. Finally, Martha Custis agreed to marry him. They lived a happy life together.

Author's Purpose: _____

Reason: _____

Name: _____

Determining The Author's Purpose

Directions: Read each paragraph. Tell whether they inform, entertain or persuade. One paragraph does more than one. Then write your reason on the line below:

A llama (LAH' MUH) is a South American animal that is related to the camel. It is raised for its wool. Also, it can carry heavy loads. Some people who live near mountains in the United States train llamas to go on mountain trips. Llamas are sure-footed because they have two long toes and toenails.

Author's Purpose: _____

Reason: _____

_____

Llama's are the best animals to have if you're planning to back-pack in the mountains. They can climb easily and carry your supplies. No one should ever go for a long hiking trip in the mountains without a llama.

Author's Purpose: _____

Reason: _____

_____

Llamas can be stubborn animals. Sometimes they suddenly stop walking for no reason. People have to push them to get them moving again. Stubborn llamas can be frustrating when hiking up a steep mountain.

Author's Purpose: _____

Reason: _____

_____

Greg is an 11-year-old boy who raises llamas to climb mountains. One of his llamas is named Dallas. Although there are special saddles for llamas, Greg likes to ride bareback.

Author's Purpose: _____

Reason: _____

_____

Now use a separate sheet of paper to inform readers about llamas.

Name: _____

Determining The Author's Purpose

Directions: Read each paragraph. Determine the author's purpose. Is it to inform, entertain or persuade?

Cookie parties that allow you to sample a variety of cookies can be more fun than pizza parties. The cookies are not hard to bake, but they still taste great. No one should finish the sixth grade without having a cookie party with his or her friends.

Author's Purpose: _____

Reason: _____

When planning a cookie party, invite five friends. Ask each of them to bake a half dozen of their favorite cookies. You should also bake six cookies. When they arrive for the party, serve milk and other drinks.

Author's Purpose: _____

Reason: _____

Cookie parties can be funny sometimes, too. One girl who went to a cookie party said, "I burnt every cookie that I baked." She brought a package of store-bought cookies with her.

Author's Purpose: _____

Reason: _____

Make cookie invitations to invite people to your party. Use brown sheets of construction paper and cut them out in round circles so that they look like cookies. Then write your name, your address and the party's date and time on them. Put your telephone number on them, too.

Author's Purpose: _____

Reason: _____

Use a separate sheet of paper to write an entertaining passage about a cookie party.

Determining The Author's Purpose

Directions: Read each paragraph and determine the author's purpose. Then write your reasons on the line below.

Roller coaster rides are thrilling. The cars chug up the hills and then fly down them. People scream and laugh. They clutch their seats and sometimes raise their arms above their heads.

Author's Purpose: _____

Reason: _____

The first roller coasters were giant sliding boards made of ice in Russia. That was more than 300 years ago! The slides were about 70 feet high and people had to climb steep ladders to reach their tops. Riders got into carts and slid down very fast. Then they climbed the ladders again. Early roller coasters were more work than fun.

Author's Purpose: _____

Reason: _____

_____

The first roller coaster in America was built in 1884. It cost only a nickel to ride the Switchback Gravity Pleasure Railway at Coney Island in New York. Roller coasters did not become very popular until the 1920s.

Author's Purpose: _____

Reason: _____

_____

Have you ever ridden a giant roller coaster? Some of the most famous ones in the world include Space Mountain at Walt Disney World in Florida, The Corkscrew at Knotts Berry Farm in California and The Demon at Six Flags Great America in Illinois. Roller coasters are fun because they have thrilling twists and turns. Some go very high and some turn upside down. Everyone should go on a roller coaster at least once in his or her life.

Author's Purpose: _____

Reason: _____

_____

On a separate sheet of paper, write a passage to persuade people to ride on roller coasters.

Determining The Author's Purpose

Directions: Read each passage about the opera composer Gioacchino Rossini. Then determine the author's purpose.

Gioacchino Rossini was born in Italy in 1792, the son of a town trumpeter and an opera singer. He learned about music and the theater from his parents. Rossini wrote his first opera, which is a drama set to music, when he was 14 years old.

Author's Purpose: _____

_____

Rossini was particular about the music he liked. "All music is good except the boring kind," he said. His own music was fast-paced and happy-sounding. Writing music came easily to Rossini. He once said, "Give me a laundry list, and I'll set it to music."

Author's Purpose: _____

The Barber of Seville was Rossini's most famous opera. It is still performed today. Rossini signed a contract to write *The Barber of Seville* the day after Christmas in 1815. He spent the next 13 days writing the opera, taking little time to eat. Rossini didn't shave during those 13 days, either. Some people said it was unusual that an opera about a barber would cause Rossini not to shave.

Author's Purpose: _____

Music is usually what people like about operas. Those who enjoy listening to music and watching plays will like operas. If you have never been to an opera, you should go.

Author's Purpose: _____

Use the information about operas to write a passage that both informs and entertains. Use a separate sheet of paper.

Name: _____

Determining The Author's Purpose

Directions: Read each paragraph about a snack you can make. Then tell the author's purpose.

Nachos with cheese are the perfect afternoon snack. They are filling and taste delicious. When you are really hungry, crispy nachos covered with warm cheese will fill you up until dinner time.

Author's Purpose: _____

_____

First, spread out 15 or 20 nacho chips on a microwave-safe plate. Then sprinkle one cup of cheddar cheese over the chips. Put the plate into the microwave oven. Cook them on high for about 30 to 45 seconds.

Author's Purpose: _____

One boy who likes nacho chips with cheese wanted to try something different. He put peanut butter on each nacho. "But when the nachos got hot, all the peanut butter ran off," he said. "So, I had to eat plain nachos and use my finger to get the peanut butter off of the plate."

Author's Purpose: _____

Nachos are a healthful snack. They are nutritious and not too sweet. If you get tired of nachos and cheese, try dipping the chips into potato chip dip before eating them. For a Mexican treat, spread taco sauce on nachos before you cook them. You can fix nachos many different ways. Buy a bag today.

Author's Purpose: _____

On a separate sheet of paper, write a passage about nachos that both informs and persuades.

Name: _____

Determining The Author's Purpose

Directions: Read each paragraph.
Then identify the author's purpose.

You have seen surfers on television, in movies or at the beach. You have also heard surfing music. When surfing is mentioned, you probably think of the sand, the ocean and the hot sun. But most of all, you probably think about the surfers who ride the waves, gliding on each one until it splashes on shore.

Author's Purpose: _____

Anyone who hasn't ridden a surf board, should try it. There's nothing like the anticipation of a 20-foot wave when you see it approaching the spot where you're standing. There's nothing like the cool spray of the ocean water as you ride along the top of the waves. Afterward, there's nothing like knowing that you've conquered the biggest wave on the beach that day.

Author's Purpose: _____

Tom Curren is a professional surfer. He began surfing with his father when he was 6 years old. When he turned 14, he started winning surfing contests. Tom Curren was named a world surfing champion in 1986 and 1987. He was the first American to win the title.

Author's Purpose: _____

Surfing isn't easy. People who surf must know how to handle the board so that they don't get hurt and they must have good timing to catch oncoming waves. Surfers are athletic people who are good swimmers.

Author's Purpose: _____

On a separate sheet of paper, write a passage about surfing that either informs, entertains or persuades.

Name: _____

Review

Directions: Read each passage about rattlesnakes. Then determine the author's purpose.

Rattlesnakes are some of the most poisonous snakes in the world. Although there are several different kinds, the most dangerous rattlesnakes are in South America and on Mexico's west coast. Rattlesnakes poison people and animals by biting them with their large, hollow fangs. But they usually bite only when they are surprised or scared.

Author's Purpose: _____

If you hear a rattlesnake's rattle, watch out. The noise is caused by dry joints of skin at the end of the snake's tail. The rattle, which you can sometimes hear 100 feet away, warns that a snake is nearby. If you hear one, turn around and walk the other direction.

Author's Purpose: _____

Luke went to the desert on vacation one year. While shopping, he noticed that rattles from rattlesnakes were only $2. Luke bought one. He couldn't wait to hide behind a desert cactus and shake it.

Author's Purpose: _____

Rattlesnakes have different kinds of poison, or venom. Some venoms make the skin numb. Others clot the blood and block veins. Some venoms cause blood cells to quit working. But venoms also help rattlesnakes digest their food.

Author's Purpose: _____

On a separate sheet of paper, write a passage about rattlesnakes that informs, entertains, persuades or combines all three author's purposes.

Name: _____

Fact Or Opinion?

A fact is something that can be proved. An opinion is a belief not necessarily based on facts.

Dolphins

(**1**) Dolphins are mammals. (**2**) They have teeth, they breathe air and they are warm-blooded. (**3**)They can also grow to be up to 10 feet long. (**4**) I think that dolphins like people because sometimes they play around ships. (**5**) But they probably like other dolphins better. (**6**) They always swim in groups with up to 100 others. (**7**) Scientists have discovered that dolphins communicate with each other by making different sounds. (**8**) That is amazing! (**9**) I think that they probably say a lot of interesting things to each other. (**10**) Dolphins are now being studied to find out how they "talk" underwater.

Directions: After reading the numbered sentences about dolphins, write in the corresponding numbered blanks whether each sentence gives a fact or an opinion.

1. _____fact_____
2. _____
3. _____
4. _____
5. _____
6. _____
7. _____
8. _____
9. _____
10. _____

Name: _____

Fact Or Opinion?

Jaws, the Movie

(1) In 1975, a movie was made about a shark that attacked people. (2) It was called *Jaws*. (3) Since then there have been four sequels. (4) I think the first movie was the best one ever made.

(5) The movie featured three main characters: the sheriff, who was afraid to allow people to swim in the ocean; the scientist, who came to town to study the huge creature; and a fisherman, who volunteered to kill the shark. (6) All three of these men were very good actors.

(7) I think the first *Jaws* movie was definitely the scariest. (8) It showed how the people of the town were afraid to swim because of the shark. (9) It showed the three men out on the boat trying to capture the beast. (10) Many people who saw the movie more than once said it was the best movie produced that summer.

Directions: After reading the numbered sentences about a movie called *Jaws*, write in the corresponding blanks whether each sentence gives a fact or an opinion.

1. _____
2. _____
3. _____
4. _____
5. _____
6. _____
7. _____
8. _____
9. _____
10. _____

Telling Fact From Opinion

John Logie Baird was the first person to demonstrate a television. Baird was born in Scotland and studied at two colleges there. Then he moved to England where he continued his research. In 1924 he showed people an image of something outlined on a screen. Baird was probably the smartest man alive at that time.

Opinion: _____

_____

In 1925 Baird showed a picture of human faces on a television picture. The television screen was beginning to get more detail in it, thanks to more research by Baird. I think people were very happy when such a discovery was made.

Opinion: _____

_____

Through the years, Baird continued his research. In 1928 he demonstrated colored television. But colored television sets were not available to the public until about 35 years later. Watching colored television was better than going to the theater.

Opinion: _____

_____

Today people know what those on the other side of the world are doing because of the television. Communication networks have gotten more powerful so that we can see events happening in other countries. If it weren't for John Baird's research, I think we would all read more books.

Opinion: _____

_____

Name: _____

Fact Or Opinion?

Movie Maker Videos

(**1**) We think you should visit Movie Maker Videos today. (**2**) We carry the largest selection of movies in the city. (**3**) Our shelves are loaded with the best comedies, dramas and adventure films on earth! (**4**) We think Movie Maker Videos is the best store in town.

(**5**) We alphabetize all our movies, according to their titles. (**6**) You won't have to spend hours looking for flicks. (**7**) Use our handy computer system to learn if a movie has been checked out. (**8**) You'll like us so much that you won't want to go anywhere else.

(**9**) At Movie Maker Videos we stock 2,000 films. (**10**) You will be happy you came to see us first. (**11**) We charge only $3.50 a night to rent a movie. (**12**) Visit Movie Maker Videos at 22 Sawville Road in Bloomington.

Directions: After reading the following advertisement for a video rental store, write in the corresponding numbered blank whether each sentence gives a fact or an opinion.

1. _____
2. _____
3. _____
4. _____
5. _____
6. _____
7. _____
8. _____
9. _____
10. _____
11. _____
12. _____

Name: _____

Fact Or Opinion?

Directions: Read about chilies and peppers. Find the one opinion in each passage.

Chilies are hot or sweet peppers. They are part of the "nightshade" family of plants that also includes potatoes and tomatoes. Potatoes and tomatoes taste better than chilies, though.

Opinion: _____

_____

Chilies were originally grown in Central and South America. By the 15th century, Europeans were cooking with them and drying them to use as a spice. European dishes taste better now than they did before chilies were used in them.

Opinion: _____

_____

Although it is really a Mexican recipe, every intelligent American loves chili con carne. It is made with spicy meat, beans and chilies. Today most Americans call that dish "chili."

Opinion: _____

_____

Some people think that all chilies are hot. Therefore, they never eat any of them. What a silly belief! There are many different kinds of red, yellow and green chilies. Even red chilies can be sweet.

Opinion: _____

_____

Name: _____

Fact Or Opinion?

Carol's Country Restaurant

(**1**) I have visited Carol's Country Restaurant seven times in the past two weeks. (**2**) The meals there are excellent. (**3**) They often feature country dishes such as meatloaf, ham and scalloped potatoes and fried chicken.

(**4**) Owner Carol Murphy makes wonderful vegetable soup that includes all home-grown vegetables. (**5**) It's simmered with thin egg noodles. (**6**) Another of my favorite dishes is Carol's chili. (**7**) I'm sure it is the spiciest chili this side of the Mississippi River. (**8**) Carol says she uses secret ingredients in all of her dishes.

(**9**) Whether ordering a main dish or a dessert, you can't go wrong at Carol's. (**10**) Everything is superb.

(**11**) Carol's Country Restaurant is on Twig Street in Freeport. (**12**) Prices for main entrees range from $2.50 to $5.95.

Directions: After reading the numbered sentences about Carol's Country Restaurant, write in the corresponding numbered blanks whether each sentence gives a fact or an opinion.

1. _____
2. _____
3. _____
4. _____
5. _____
6. _____
7. _____
8. _____
9. _____
10. _____
11. _____
12. _____

Fact Or Opinion?

Thunderbird Jets

(1) The United States Air Force Thunderbirds are a group of red, white and blue jets that do shows for people. (2) The Thunderbirds do special kinds of stunts. (3) Their performances are awesome.

(4) One stunt, called the arrowhead roll, is when four jets form a huge arch in the sky. (5) It is an amazing trick! (6) The planes fly only a few feet apart.

(7) One of the Thunderbird's jets is called the F-16 Fighting Falcon. (8) Through the years there have been many planes that were included in the Thunderbirds. (9) Regardless of what they fly, this Airforce team is delightful.

(10) The Air Force specially trains pilots who fly these jets. (11) Before they can go on the Thunderbird team, the pilots have to have flown a jet fighter for at least 1,000 hours. (12) Being a Thunderbird pilot is the most exciting job on earth!

Directions: After reading the numbered sentences about Thunderbird Jets, write in the corresponding numbered blanks whether each sentence gives a fact or an opinion.

1. _____

2. _____

3. _____

4. _____

5. _____

6. _____

7. _____

8. _____

9. _____

10. _____

11. _____

12. _____

Review

The Thunderbirds Fly Again

(**1**) People attending Sunday's 13th annual Dayton Air Show roared with approval when the Air Force Thunderbird jets were spotted off in the distance.

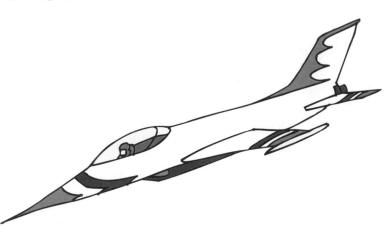

(**2**) But since Sunday's show, it seems people have been less enthusiastic about the Thunderbird jets. (**3**) This reporter believes the sky was the brightest blue it had been in weeks. (**4**) The planes belched gray smoke into it. (**5**) The jets were too noisy, too. (**6**) Residents for miles around could hear them for the entire hour that they performed.

(**7**) Admittedly, the Thunderbirds gave an astounding performance when the six red, white and blue planes zoomed by the crowd. (**8**) I think that maybe it's time that air show officials plan a different program. (**9**) There were fewer people at Sunday's show than in previous years. (**10**) Perhaps the people in Dayton have grown tired of the Thunderbird jets.

Directions: After reading the numbered sentences about one performance of the Thunderbird Jets, write in the corresponding numbered blanks whether each sentence gives a fact or an opinion.

1. _____

2. _____

3. _____

4. _____

5. _____

6. _____

7. _____

8. _____

9. _____

10. _____

Preparing For And Taking Tests

Multiple-choice questions are frequently on tests. Such questions include three or four possible answers. When answering a multiple-choice question, first read the question carefully. Then read all of the answers that are offered. If you do not know the correct answer, eliminate some of the ones that you know are wrong until you have only one left.

Remember these points when taking multiple-choice tests:

1. Answers that contain phrases such as **all people, no one** or **everybody** are probably not correct. For example, a sentence such as "all children like candy" is probably not correct because it allows for no exceptions. If there is one child who does not like candy, the statement is not right. However, if you know that more than one answer is right and the last choice in the group is "all of the above," then that phrase is probably the correct answer.

2. Answers that contain words you have never seen before probably are not correct. Teachers don't expect you to know material that you haven't studied.

3. Answers that are silly usually aren't correct.

4. When two of the answers provided look nearly the same, one of them is probably correct.

5. Always check your answers if there is time.

Directions: After reading about tests that have multiple-choice questions on them, follow the instructions.

1. Tests frequently have _____ questions on them.

2. The first thing you should do during a multiple choice test is

_____ .

3. When you are reading the possible answers to a multiple-choice question and you know the first one is right, should you immediately mark it without reading the other answers? Why or why not? _____

_____

4. Write three phrases that could tell you that an answer is probably not correct.

_____

5. If the phrase _____ is used as the last answer on a test, it is probably the right one.

Name: _____

Preparing For And Taking Tests

True — false tests include several statements. You must read each one carefully to determine if it is right or wrong. Remember these tips:

1. Watch for one word in the sentence that can change the statement's meaning from true to false or vice versa.

2. Words such as **all, none, everybody** or **nobody** should alert you that the answer may be false. For example, using the word **everybody** means that there are no exceptions.

3. There are usually more true answers than false ones. Therefore, if you have to guess an answer, you have a better chance of getting the statement right by marking it true.

4. Always check your answers if there is time.

Directions: Answer the questions about true — false tests.

1. List four words that can alert you that a question is false:

_____

2. One word in a sentence can

_____ .

3. If you must guess an answer, is it wiser to guess true or false? _____

4. True — false tests are made up of several _____ .

5. Can you do well on a true — false test by only skimming each statement? _____

6. If the word "everybody" is in the statement, is the answer probably true or false?   _____

7. When the word "all" appears in a statement, is the answer probably true or false?   _____

8. What should you do last when taking a true — false test?

_____

Preparing For And Taking Tests

Fill-in-the-blank tests are more difficult than true — false or multiple-choice tests. However, there may be clues in each sentence that help determine the answer. Look at this example:

The _____ of the United States serves a _____ -year term.

Can you tell that the first blank needs the name of a person? (The answer is "President.") The second blank needs a number because it refers to years. ("Four" is the answer.) Think about these other tips for taking fill-in-the-blank tests:

1. Always plan your time wisely. Don't waste too much time on one question. Check the clock or your watch periodically when taking a test.

2. First read through the entire test. Then go back to the beginning and answer the questions that you know. Put a small mark beside the questions that you are not sure about.

3. Go back to the questions you were not sure of or that you didn't know. Carefully read each one. Think about possible answers. If you think it could be more than one answer, try to eliminate some of the possible answers.

4. Save the most difficult questions to answer last. Don't waste time worrying if you don't know the answer to a question.

5. Sometimes you should guess at an answer because it may be right. There are some tests, though, that deduct points if your answer is wrong, but not if it is left blank. Make sure you know how the test will be scored.

6. Review your test. Make sure you have correctly read the directions and each question. Check your answers.

Directions: After reading the tips about tests in which you have to fill in the blank, answer each question.

1. Fill-in-the-blank tests may have _____ in each sentence that help you figure out the answer.

2. Always plan your _____ wisely when taking a test.

3. Should you try to answer every question as soon as you read it?   _____

4. Should you answer the hard or easy questions first?   _____

5. If you are not sure of a question, you should _____
   beside it.

Preparing For And Taking Tests

Matching tests have two columns of information. A word or fact from one column matches information in the other. Read these tips to help with matching tests:

1. Look at one question at a time. Start with the first word or phrase in one of the columns. Then look at the possible answers in the other column until you find the correct one. Then go to the next word or phrase in the first column. If you don't know the answer to one question, skip it and go back to it later.

2. If there are several words in one column and several definitions in the other column, it is often easier to read the definition first and then find the word that goes with it.

3. Carefully read the directions. Sometimes one column on a matching test is longer than the other. Find out if there is one answer that won't be used or if an answer in the opposite column can be used twice.

4. Check your answers if there is time.

Directions: Answer the following questions about matching tests.

1. Matching tests have how many columns of information? _____

2. If one column has words in it and the other column has definitions in it, which one should you look at first to make taking the test easier?

_____

3. To eliminate confusion, you should look at _____ question at a time.

4. Do the columns in a matching test always have the same number of things in them? _____

5. If one column has one more item in it than the other, should you automatically use one answer in the shorter column two times? _____

6. Are there ever items left unmatched in a matching test?

_____

7. Does it matter if you look at the right or the left column of a matching test first? _____

Preparing For And Taking Tests

Essay questions give you a chance to demonstrate what you have learned. They also provide the opportunity to express your opinion. Although many students think essay questions are the most difficult, they can be the most fun. Remember these tips when writing the answer to an essay question: **1**. Think about the answer before you write it. Take time to organize your thoughts so that you can better express yourself. **2**. Write a few notes or an outline on a piece of scrap paper or on the back of the test. This helps remind you what you want to write. **3**. State answers clearly. Don't forget to use complete sentences. **4**. Review the answer before time runs out. Sometimes words are left out. It doesn't take much time to read through your answer to make sure it says what you want it to say.

Directions: Use these essay writing tips to answer the following question in the space provided:

What is your favorite type of test? Give several reasons why.

Name: _____

Review

Directions: Complete each question about tests.

1. Four steps for writing an essay test include:

1) _____

2) _____

3) _____

4) _____

2. In a matching test, it is sometimes easier to read the _____ and then match it with a word from the opposite column.

3. One column in a _____ may be longer than the other.

4. Tests that require you to fill in the blanks may provide_____ in each statement.

5. Always _____ answers if there is time.

6. Certain words such as **none** and **all** should alert you that an answer may be _____.

7. There are usually, but not always, more_____ statements on a true — false test.

8. If **everybody** or **everything** is used in one of the answers for a _____

_____, it is likely that that answer is not right.

9. If two possible answers for a multiple-choice question sound nearly the _____ , one of them is probably correct.

10. If two answers to a multiple-choice question appear to be correct, the answer could be one that says _____ .

Web of the Senses

Would you like to learn a different way of taking notes?
Start by reading this passage.

You know what your five senses are: sight, taste, touch, hearing, and smell. The most mysterious is probably smell. Scientists are not completely sure about how smell works. They do know, however, that smell is closely related to memory. The smell of something, such as chalk dust, can bring back strong memories. The chalk dust may make you think of your first grade teacher or a time you had to clean all the erasers after school.

Here are some things that are known about the mechanism of smell. You detect smells by breathing air that carries odors. Odors come from tiny particles called molecules that are given off by many substances. These molecules stimulate special cells inside your nose. Tiny hairlike nerve endings, about ten million in each nostril, pick up signals from these cells and rush messages to your brain. Your brain then sorts out these messages and "tells" you what you are smelling.

Now look at the web below. Complete the top part with the names of the missing senses.

Now complete the bottom part to show what the article says about how smell works.

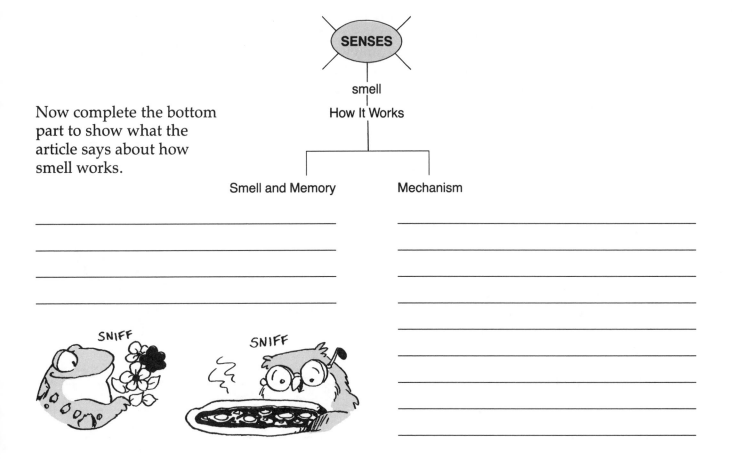

SENSES

smell

How It Works

Smell and Memory   Mechanism

SNIFF   SNIFF

What Next?

Read each story beginning.
Decide what will happen next.
Write your ideas on the lines provided.
If you need more room to write, use a separate sheet of paper.

The girls and boys stood in a tight knot, whispering and often laughing. Every once in a while, Nanette could hear Carl's loud booming laugh or Rosa's hiccupping giggle. A couple of times, Tommy looked over at her, grinning. Were they laughing at her? Why? Suddenly the bus was there, and its doors wheezed open. The knot untied itself as the boys and girls threaded their way onto the bus. Nanette sighed. Before she could even get herself to begin crossing the street, the doors started to close.

What happened next? _____

_____

_____

The lion crept toward the antelope, moving perhaps an inch at a time. It had to close the distance between them so that the final pounce would be on target. Meanwhile, the antelope grazed peacefully. Was it aware of the lion? Or was it just leading the lion on? It seemed to be tensing its back leg muscles, getting ready for a leap of its own.

What happened next? _____

_____

_____

We gathered around the smoking rock, or whatever it was. It had come down like a flaming streak through the night sky and landed in the vacant lot next to my home. Jane wanted to go right up to it and bang it with a stick, but it was too hot to get that close. So Miguel threw a rock at it. Suddenly a crack appeared, and a fierce red light shone out through it. Then the crack began to widen.

What happened next? _____

_____

_____

Predicting outcomes

Capture the Story

Here is a little challenge.
Choose one of the stories listed in the box, or use some other story you know well.
Try to "capture" the story by writing a summary of it in just three sentences.

The Three Little Pigs	The Boston Tea Party	The Hare and the Tortoise
The Story of Columbus	Hansel and Gretel	The Ugly Duckling
The Tale of Peter Rabbit	Snow White and the Seven Dwarfs	The California Gold Rush

Three-Sentence Summary

_____

_____

_____

_____

_____

_____

_____

_____

Here is a stiffer challenge.
Try to write an even shorter summary of the story you just summarized in three sentences.
See if you can "capture" the story in just one sentence.
Here is an example for "Goldilocks and the Three Bears."

While the three bears were out for a walk, Goldilocks entered their home, made a general mess of things, and then fell asleep.

One-Sentence Summary

_____

_____

_____

Now read your one-sentence summary to a classmate.
See if she or he can identify the story.
If not, read your classmate your three-sentence summary.
Have your classmate try again to identify the story.

Writing a plot summary

Comic Order

Here is an activity for you and a friend.
Cut out two comic strips from a newspaper, or use parts of two stories from a comic book you do not mind cutting up.
Cut apart the panels of each strip.
Have your friend do the same.
Then give each other one panel from each of your comic strips.
Mix all the remaining panels together and lay them out face up.
Take turns choosing panels from the group that go with the panels you already have.
When all the panels have been chosen, arrange the panels of your strips in order.
Then decide which completed comic strip you both like best and paste it below.
On the lines at the bottom of the page, write a two-sentence summary of what happened in the strip.

What's Wrong?

Look at the picture below.
Use what you know about the world you live in to figure out what is wrong with it.
Color all the things you find that just cannot be true.

How many things did you find? _____

How did you do?   0–5   Look some more.   11–15   Great!
                   6–10   Pretty good.   16 or more   Fantastic!

Using prior knowledge

Sort It Out

A fact is something that can be counted, measured, or checked.
You may not be able to count or measure some things yourself,
but someone has counted or measured them.
An opinion is what someone thinks or feels about something.
It cannot be counted, measured, or checked.
Below is a machine that sorts out facts and opinions.
Read each sentence and mark it **F** for *fact* or **O** for *opinion*.
Then "run" the sentences through the machine.
Write the number of each fact sentence in the part of the Fact
Bin that describes how someone proved the fact.
Write the number of each opinion sentence in the Opinion Bin.

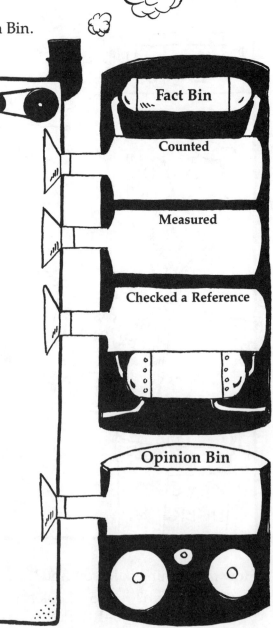

1. _____ The smallest frog ever found was only an inch long.

2. _____ Bananas taste better than apples or pears.

3. _____ There has never been a war in Switzerland.

4. _____ The little girl has 20 baby teeth.

5. _____ The best car ever built was the 1919 Stutz.

6. _____ The average speed of an ocean liner is 33 miles per hour.

7. _____ The first successful typewriter was invented in 1867.

8. _____ The stadium holds 100,001 spectators.

9. _____ Few birds are as beautiful as the flamingo.

10. _____ The tallest waterfall in the world drops 3212 feet.

11. _____ The word *run* has 250 different meanings in English.

12. _____ In 1957, the Russians launched the first Earth satellite.

13. _____ Coin collecting is an exciting and fun hobby.

14. _____ Potatoes consist of about 80 per cent water.

Identifying facts and opinions

Who's Telling?

Read each paragraph below.
Decide who is telling the story.

A A character in the story.
   The story is seen through this character's eyes and tells
   this character's feelings and reactions to the story.

B A narrator who is not a character in the story.
   This narrator sees more than any one character could.

C A narrator who is also a character in the story.
   This narrator is often referred to by the word *I*.

Write **A**, **B**, or **C** in front of each paragraph to show who is
telling the story.

____ I could feel the crunch of the gravel under my boots as I
hiked up the driveway. Uncle Bill and Aunt Lillian served the best
food in the world, though they did not realize how much I liked it.
They thought all I liked was pizza and burgers, but they always
invited me anyway. It was really no hardship to make the trip to
their house every Sunday for supper.

____ Jared turned the object over and over in his hand. "Smooth
yet rough. Heavy one minute and light the next," he muttered to
himself. He looked up and saw the alien come through the hatch
of the spacecraft. His face felt hot as the alien cackled, "I see you
have found our little toy."

____ Martine leaped onto the horse. "Let's go!" she shouted, and
a thousand head of cattle started thundering amid the yips and
whistles of the cowhands. It was a bright, clear day, and no one
sensed that by nightfall they would be in a raging blizzard.

____ The robot glided into the room on whispering rubber tires. It
turned this way and that, trying to get a fix on where things were
so it would not run into them. Yolanda smiled. Everything seemed
to be going according to plan. Then I picked up a ball and threw it
to the robot.

____ Rudolph's heart was pounding so hard he thought it might
jump right out of his chest. Could this really be what he had
wanted and worked so hard for? He brushed the hair from his
forehead. Then, his crutches creaking slightly under his hands, he
walked up to accept the award.

Identifying a story's point of view

Sound Blaster

An author writes with a purpose.
An author's purpose may be to

Inform (give the reader facts and information),
Entertain (amuse the reader), or
Persuade (convince the reader to do something or share an opinion).

Read each paragraph below.
Circle **I**, **E**, or **P** to show whether the author's *main* purpose is to inform, entertain, or persuade.

I **E** **P**	You won't believe your ears! The new Sound Blaster presents the absolute end in sound reproduction. Sound so real you can reach out and touch it! Rush down to your dealer today. Prepare to be blasted away! Then take home this wonderful little marvel for just $29.95 (plus tax).

I **E** **P**	Evelyn put down the new Sound Blaster on the table. She put in a tape, pressed a button, flopped down on her bed, and closed her eyes. Suddenly the room was filled with an unbelievably loud sound. Evelyn's head jerked up and her eyes popped open. She found herself—where?—sliding down the inside of a slippery, bright golden cone. It was a saxophone!

I **E** **P**	In our examination of the new Sound Blaster, we found the usual audio system parts. There were standard transistors and tuning circuits, a tape drive, good quality amplifiers, and easy-to-use controls. The one unusual part was a small black box located in one corner. The box was completely sealed and impossible to open. It must be the secret to the Sound Blaster's superior performance, which is achieved without the use of separate speakers.

I **E** **P**	Can you believe it? Teenagers all over the country are reporting being transported by their own music systems. Take Doug Johnson, for example. This fourteen-year-old from Passadel was admitted to General Hospital last Friday wide-eyed and babbling about being kidnapped by a bass drum. And then there is Evelyn Ullman of Flin Park, who claims she woke up inside a saxophone. In these cases, and others, the youngsters had been playing the latest model Sound Blaster. There must be something magical about the new model. It is literally taking over everyone on the teenage music scene.

Would you like to own the latest model Sound Blaster?   _____ yes   _____ no

Why? _____

Identifying the author's purpose

ANSWER KEY

MASTER THINKING SKILLS
6

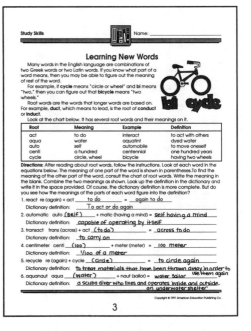

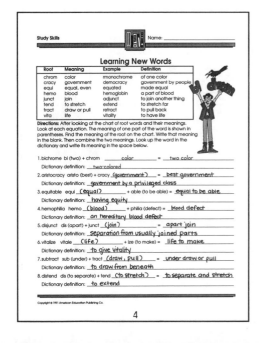

Page 5

Learning New Words From Their Prefixes And Roots

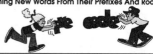

Root	Meaning	Example	Definition
cede	to go	supercede	to go beyond
cept	seize	intercept	to seize during
ducel	ead	deduce	to find the lead
fere	carry	interfere	to carry into
port	carry	transport	to carry across
spect	to look	inspect	to look in
tain	to hold	obtain	to gain by or action
vene	to come	convene	to come to start

Directions: After looking at the chart of root words and their meanings. Look at each word below. The meaning of one part of the word is shown in parentheses. Find the meaning of the other part on the chart. Write it in the blank. Combine the two meanings. Look up the meaning in the dictionary and write it in the space provided.

1. precede pre (before) + cede __to go__ = __before to go__
   Dictionary definition: __to be, go or come ahead__
2. report re (again) + port (carry) = __again carry__
   Dictionary definition: __to present an account of__
3. intervene inter (between) + vene (to come) = __between to come.__
   Dictionary definition: __to be or come between things__
4. induce in (in) + duce (lead) = __in lead__
   Dictionary definition: __to lead on__
5. retrospect retro (again) + spect (to look) = __again to look__
   Dictionary definition: __to look back at__
6. refer re (again) + fere (carry) = __again carry__
   Dictionary definition: __to send or direct toward information__
7. retain re (again) + tain (to hold) = __to hold again__
   Dictionary definition: __to hold back__
8. concept con (with) + cept (seize) = __with seize.__
   Dictionary definition: __something conceived in the mind__

5

Page 6

Learning New Words

A prefix is a syllable at the beginning of a word that changes its meaning. By knowing the meaning of a prefix, you may be able to figure out the meaning of a word. For example, the prefix **pre** means "before." That could help you figure out that **preschool** means "before school."

Directions: After reading about prefixes and their roots, follow the instructions.

A. Look at each word. Write its prefix and its base word. The prefixes **a-, im-, in-, non-,** and **un** mean "not."

Word	Prefix	Base Word
amoral	a-	moral
impractical	im-	practical
indirect	in-	direct
nonsense	non-	sense
unaffected	un-	affected

B. Use a word from the chart above to complete each sentence.

1. A person who does not have good ethics is sometimes called __amoral__

2. If two sailors went through a storm at sea and survived, they could be __unaffected__ by it.

3. A comedian who makes many jokes sometimes talks __nonsense__

4. To carry an umbrella on a sunny day is __impractical__

5. Buying flowers is an __indirect__ way of saying, "I love you."

6

Page 7

Learning New Words

Directions: The prefixes **co-, col-, com-, con-,** and **cor-** mean "with or together." The prefixes **anti-, contra-** and **ob-** mean "against." Use that information to complete the exercises below.

A. Read each word. Write its prefix and base word in the space provided.

Word	Prefix	Base Word
coexist	co-	exist
concurrent	con-	current
correlate	cor-	relate
codependent	co-	dependent
antigravity	anti-	gravity
contraband	contra-	band

B. Use the words above to complete the sentences.

1. When airplanes fly very high and then quickly drop down, they cause an __antigravity__ affect.

2. Materials that are illegal are called __contraband__

3. A dog and a cat can __coexist__ in the same house if they get along well.

4. Events that happen at the same time are __concurrent__

5. When two people rely on each other, they are said to be __codependent__

6. The text book will __correlate__ with the teacher's lectures.

7

Page 8

Learning New Words

Directions: The prefixes **epi-, hyper-, over-** and **super-** mean "above or over." The prefixes **under-** and **sub-** mean "under." Follow the instructions for each question.

A. Read each word. Write its prefix and base word in the space provided.

Word	Prefix	Root
hyperactive	hyper-	active
overanxious	over-	anxious
superimpose	super-	impose
epilogue	epi-	logue
underestimate	under-	estimate
subordinate	sub-	ordinate

B. Use the words above to complete the following sentences.

1. A photographer could __superimpose__ one image on top of another.

2. The __epilogue__ of the book may tell additional information about the story.

3. All the other children settled down for the night, except the boy who was __hyperactive__.

4. He could not sleep because he was __overanxious__ about the upcoming trip.

5. The company's president told his __subordinate__ to take over some of the responsibilities.

6. Just because you think you are weak, don't __underestimate__ how strong you could be.

8

Page 9

Learning New Words

Directions: Some prefixes are related to numbers. For example, in Latin **uni** means "one." The prefix **mono** means "one" in Greek. Look at the chart below. It lists prefixes for numbers one through 10 from both the Latin and Greek languages.

Number	Latin	Example	Greek	Example
1	uni	university	mon, mono	monopoly
2	du	duplex	di	digress
3	tri	tricycle	tri	tricycle
4	quad	quadrant	tetro	tetrameter
5	quin	quintuplets	penta	pentagonquar
6	sex	sexennial	hex	hexagon
7	sept	September	hept	heptagon
8	oct	October	oct	octagon
9	nov	November	enne	ennead (group of nine)
10	dec	decade	dec	decade

Look at each word in the equation below. The meaning of one part of the word is shown in parentheses. To find the meaning of the other part of the word, consult the chart. Write the meaning in the blank. Combine the two meanings as shown in the example. Look up the definition in the dictionary and write it in the space provided.

1. unicycle uni (one) + cycle (wheel) = __one wheel__
   Dictionary definition: __various single-wheeled vehicles__
2. monogram mono (one) + gram (writing) = __one writing__
   Dictionary definition: __a sign of identity formed with combined initials__
3. sextet sex (six) + tet (group) = __six group__
   Dictionary definition: __a set or group of six__
4. quad quad (four) + rant (part) = __four part__
   Dictionary definition: __any one of four parts__
5. hexagonal hex (six) + agonal (angle) = __six angle__
   Dictionary definition: __having six angles or six sides__
6. trialogue tri (three) + alogue (to speak) = __three to speak__
   Dictionary definition: __a scene that three people share__
7. octave oct (eight) + ave (to have) = __eight to have__
   Dictionary definition: __a group of eight__
8. decigram dec (ten) + gram (gram) = __ten grams__
   Dictionary definition: __one tenth of a gram__

9

Page 10

Review

Directions: Read each question. Follow the instructions.
A. Look at the box of the roots and the prefixes with their meanings. Then look at each equation. Write the meaning of each part of the word in the space provided. Then combine the meanings. Look up the word in a dictionary. Write its meaning.

Roots	Meanings	Prefixes	Meanings
fere	carry	dis	separate
graph	to write	epi	upon, above
rupt	break	ex	out
tend	stretch	in	in
vade	to go	trans	across

1. invade in __in__ + vade __to go__ = __in to go__
   Definition: __to go in__
2. disrupt dis (separate) + rupt (break) = __separate break__
   Definition: __to break between__
3. transfer trans (across) + fere (carry) = __across carry__
   Definition: __to carry across__
4. extend ex (out) + tend (stretch) = __outstretch__
   Definition: __to stretch out__
5. epigraph epi (upon) + graph (to write) = __upon to write__
   Definition: __to write above__

B. The prefixes **mono-** and **uni-** both mean "one." Look at each word. Write its prefix and its root in the space provided. Then complete each sentence with one of the words from the chart.

Word	Prefix	Root
monorhyme	mono-	rhyme
monosyllable	mono-	syllable
unilingual	uni-	lingual
uniparental	uni-	parental

1. We went on a camping trip with my father. __uniparental__
2. The Mexican children were __unilingual__
3. Words at the ends of each line in a sound similar. __monorhyme__
4. "Cat" is an example of a __monosyllable__

10

Page 11

Using New Words

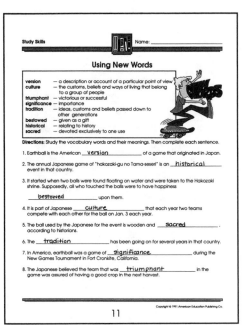

version	— a description or account of a particular point of view
culture	— the customs, beliefs and ways of living that belong to a group of people
triumphant	— victorious or successful
significance	— importance
tradition	— ideas, customs and beliefs passed down to other generations
bestowed	— given as a gift
historical	— relating to history
sacred	— devoted exclusively to one use

Directions: Study the vocabulary words and their meanings. Then complete each sentence.

1. Earthball is the American __version__ of a game that originated in Japan.
2. The annual Japanese game of "hakozaki-gu no Tama-seseri" is an __historical__ event in that country.
3. It started when two balls were found floating on water and were taken to the Hakozaki shrine. Supposedly, all who touched the balls were to have happiness __bestowed__ upon them.
4. It is part of Japanese __culture__ that each year two teams compete with each other for the ball on Jan. 3 each year.
5. The ball used by the Japanese for the event is wooden and __sacred__, according to historians.
6. The __tradition__ has been going on for several years in that country.
7. In America, earthball was a game of __significance__ during the New Games Tournament in Fort Cronkite, California.
8. The Japanese believed the team that was __triumphant__ in the game was assured of having a good crop in the next harvest.

Page 14

Using New Words

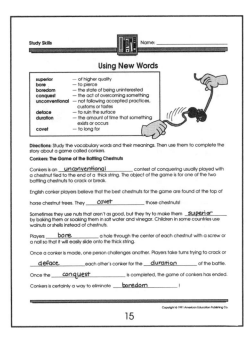

vigorous	— full of energy, lively
rival	— competitor
primary	— first or foremost
technique	— a method by which a task is carried out
devise	— to think of, plan or invent
characteristically	— having the usual qualities
catapult	— to throw
function	— purpose or use

Directions: Study the vocabulary words and their meanings. Then complete each sentence in the story about hoop games.

Hoop Games

Hoops have been around for thousands of years. Ancient Greek doctors recommended that people use hula-hoops for __vigorous__ exercise.

Target shooting was the __primary__ reason that American Indian boys used hoops. They covered them with animal skins or woven fabric. Two lines of Indian boys faced each other and rolled the hoops back and forth. Players __catapulted__ darts at the rolling targets.

Some Eskimos used a similar __technique__ when playing hoop games, but they didn't cover their hoops. They rolled a hoop between two __rivals__ and threw long poles through the big hole.

Hoops have had different __functions__ through the years. Children in Europe liked to bowl, or roll, hoops for fun. They bowled hoops by flinging them forward and running along beside them while pushing them with sticks or the palms of their hands.

Children who play with hula-hoops still __devise__ new uses for them.

Today people __characteristically__ put hula-hoops around their waists and wriggle their bodies to spin them in circles. Doing the hula-hoop is good exercise.

Page 12

Using New Words

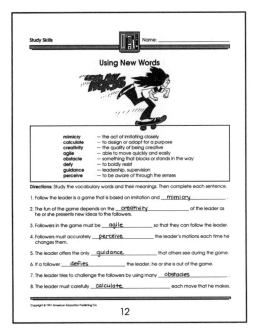

mimicry	— the act of imitating closely
calculate	— to design or adapt for a purpose
creativity	— the quality of being creative
agile	— able to move quickly and easily
obstacle	— something that blocks or stands in the way
defy	— to boldly resist
guidance	— leadership, supervision
perceive	— to be aware of through the senses

Directions: Study the vocabulary words and their meanings. Then complete each sentence.

1. Follow the leader is a game that is based on imitation and __mimicry__.
2. The fun of the game depends on the __creativity__ of the leader as he or she presents new ideas to the followers.
3. Followers in the game must be __agile__ so that they can follow the leader.
4. Followers must accurately __perceive__ the leader's motions each time he changes them.
5. The leader offers the only __guidance__ that others see during the game.
6. If a follower __defies__ the leader, he or she is out of the game.
7. The leader tries to challenge the followers by using many __obstacles__.
8. The leader must carefully __calculate__ each move that he makes.

Page 15

Using New Words

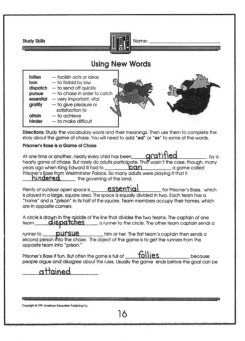

superior	— of higher quality
bore	— to pierce
boredom	— the state of being uninterested
conquest	— the act of overcoming something
unconventional	— not following accepted practices, customs or tastes
deface	— to ruin the surface
duration	— the amount of time that something exists or occurs
covet	— to long for

Directions: Study the vocabulary words and their meanings. Then use them to complete the story about a game called conkers.

Conkers: The Game of the Battling Chestnuts

Conkers is an __unconventional__ contest of conquering usually played with a chestnut tied to the end of a thick string. The object of the game is for one of the two battling chestnuts to crack or break.

English conker players believe that the best chestnuts for the game are found at the top of horse chestnut trees. They __covet__ those chestnuts!

Sometimes they use nuts that aren't as good, but they try to make them __superior__ by baking them or soaking them in salt water and vinegar. Children in some countries use walnuts or shells instead of chestnuts.

Players __bore__ a hole through the center of each chestnut with a screw or a nail so that it will easily slide onto the thick string.

Once a conker is made, one person challenges another. Players take turns trying to crack or __deface__ each other's conker for the __duration__ of the battle.

Once the __conquest__ is completed, the game of conkers has ended.

Conkers is certainly a way to eliminate __boredom__!

Page 13

Using New Words

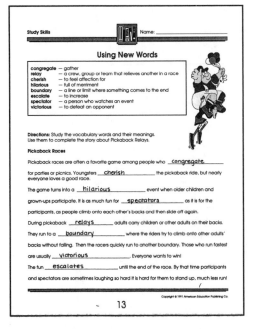

congregate	— gather
relay	— a crew, group or team that relieves another in a race
cherish	— to feel affection for
hilarious	— full of merriment
boundary	— a line or limit where something comes to the end
escalate	— to increase
spectator	— a person who watches an event
victorious	— to defeat an opponent

Directions: Study the vocabulary words and their meanings. Use them to complete the story about Pickaback Relays.

Pickaback Races

Pickaback races are often a favorite game among people who __congregate__ for parties or picnics. Youngsters __cherish__ the pickaback ride, but nearly everyone loves a good race.

The game turns into a __hilarious__ event when older children and grown-ups participate. It is much fun for __spectators__ as it is for the participants, as people climb onto each other's backs and then slide off again.

During pickaback __relays__ adults carry children or other adults on their backs.

They run to a __boundary__ where the riders try to climb onto other adults' backs without falling. Then the racers quickly run to another boundary. Those who run fastest are usually __victorious__. Everyone wants to win!

The fun __escalates__ until the end of the race. By that time participants and spectators are sometimes laughing so hard it is hard for them to stand up, much less run!

Page 16

Using New Words

follies	— foolish acts or ideas
ban	— to forbid by law
dispatch	— to send off quickly
pursue	— to chase in order to catch
essential	— very important, vital
gratify	— to give pleasure or satisfaction to
attain	— to achieve
hinder	— to make difficult

Directions: Study the vocabulary words and their meanings. Then use them to complete the story about the game of chase. You will need to add "ed" or "es" to some of the words.

Prisoner's Base is a Game of Chase

At one time or another, nearly every child has been __gratified__ by a hearty game of chase. But rarely do adults participate. That wasn't the case, though, many years ago when King Edward III had to __ban__ a game called Prisoner's Base from Westminster Palace. So many adults were playing it that it __hindered__ the governing of the land.

Plenty of outdoor open space is __essential__ for Prisoner's Base, which is played in a large, square area. The space is equally divided in two. Each team has a "home" and a "prison" in its half of the square. Team members occupy their homes, which are in opposite corners.

A circle is drawn in the middle of the line that divides the two teams. The captain of one team __dispatches__ a runner to the circle. The other team captain sends a runner to __pursue__ him or her. The first team's captain then sends a second person into the chase. The object of the game is to get the runners from the opposite team into "prison."

Prisoner's Base is certainly full of __follies__ because people argue and disagree about the rules. Usually the game ends before the goal can be __attained__.

Using New Words

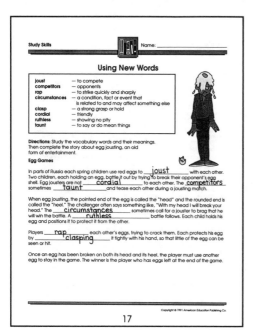

joust	— to compete
competitors	— opponents
rap	— to strike quickly and sharply
circumstances	— a condition, fact or event that is related to and may affect something else
clasp	— a strong grasp or hold
cordial	— friendly
ruthless	— showing no pity
taunt	— to say or do mean things

Directions: Study the vocabulary words and their meanings. Then complete the story about egg jousting, an old form of entertainment.

Egg Games

In parts of Russia each spring children use red eggs to __joust__ with each other. Two children, each holding an egg, battle it out by trying to break their opponent's egg shell. Egg jousters are not __cordial__ to each other. The __competitors__ sometimes __taunt__ and tease each other during a jousting match.

When egg jousting, the pointed end of the egg is called the "head" and the rounded end is called the "heel." The challenger often says something like, "With my head I will break your head." The __circumstances__ sometimes call for a jouster to brag that he will win the battle. A __ruthless__ battle follows. Each child holds his egg and positions it to protect it from the other.

Players __rap__ each other's eggs, trying to crack them. Each protects his egg by __clasping__ it tightly with his hand, so that little of the egg can be seen or hit.

Once an egg has been broken on both its head and its heel, the player must use another egg to stay in the game. The winner is the player who has eggs left at the end of the game.

17

Locating Information

Directions: The table of contents below is divided into units and sections. Units are parts into which a book is divided. Sections are segments of each unit.

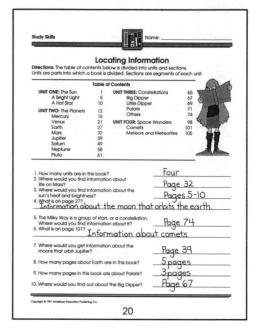

Table of Contents

UNIT ONE: The Sun	1	UNIT THREE: Constellations	65
A Bright Light	5	Big Dipper	67
A Hot Star	10	Little Dipper	69
UNIT TWO: The Planets	12	Polaris	71
Mercury	15	Others	74
Venus	21	UNIT FOUR: Space Wonders	98
Earth	27	Comets	101
Mars	32	Meteors and Meteorites	105
Jupiter	39		
Saturn	49		
Neptune	58		
Pluto	61		

1. How many units are in this book?   **Four**
2. Where would you find information about life on Mars?   **Page 32**
3. Where would you find information about the sun's heat and brightness?   **Pages 5-10**
4. What is on page 27?   **Information about the moon that orbits the earth.**
5. The Milky Way is a group of stars, or a constellation. Where would you find information about it?   **Page 74**
6. What is on page 101?   **Information about comets.**
7. Where would you get information about the moons that orbit Jupiter?   **Page 39**
8. How many pages about Earth are in this book?   **5 pages**
9. How many pages in this book are about Polaris?   **3 pages**
10. Where would you find out about the Big Dipper?   **Page 67**

20

Review

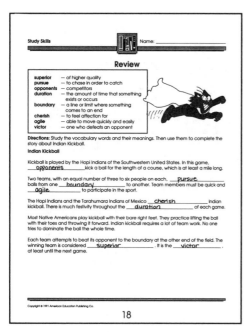

superior	— of higher quality
pursue	— to chase in order to catch
opponents	— competitors
duration	— the amount of time that something exists or occurs
boundary	— a line or limit where something comes to an end
cherish	— to feel affection for
agile	— able to move quickly and easily
victor	— one who defeats an opponent

Directions: Study the vocabulary words and their meanings. Then use them to complete the story about Indian Kickball.

Indian Kickball

Kickball is played by the Hopi Indians of the Southwestern United States. In this game, __opponents__ kick a ball for the length of a course, which is at least a mile long.

Two teams, with an equal number of three to six people on each, __pursue__ balls from one __boundary__ to another. Team members must be quick and __agile__ to participate in the sport.

The Hopi Indians and the Tarahumara Indians of Mexico __cherish__ Indian kickball. There is much festivity throughout the __duration__ of each game.

Most Native Americans play kickball with their bare right feet. They practice lifting the ball with their toes and throwing it forward. Indian kickball requires a lot of team work. No one tries to dominate the ball the whole time.

Each team attempts to beat its opponent to the boundary at the other end of the field. The winning team is considered __superior__. It is the __victor__, at least until the next game.

18

Locating Information

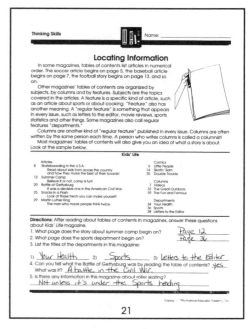

In some magazines, tables of contents list articles in numerical order. The soccer article begins on page 5, the baseball article begins on page 7, the football story begins on page 13, and so on.

Other magazines' tables of contents are organized by subjects, by columns and by features. Subjects are the topics covered in the articles. A feature is a specific kind of article, such as an article about sports or about cooking. "Feature" also has another meaning. A "regular feature" is something that appears in every issue, such as letters to the editor, movie reviews, sports statistics and other things. Some magazines also call regular features "departments".

Columns are another kind of "regular feature" published in every issue. Columns are often written by the same person each time. A person who writes columns is called a columnist.

Most magazines' tables of contents will also give you an idea of what a story is about. Look at the sample below.

Kids' Life

Articles		Comics	
8	Skateboarding in the U.S.A.	6	Little People
	Read about kids from across the country and how they make the best of their boards!	14	Skatin' Sam
12	Summer Camp	30	Double Trouble
	Believe it or not, camp is fun!		Columns
20	Battle of Gettysburg	7	Videos
	If was a decisive one in the American Civil War.	32	The Great Outdoors
25	Snacks in a Flash	39	The Fun and Famous
	Look at these treats you can make yourself!		Departments
29	Martin Luther King	34	Your Health
	The man who made more people think twice.	36	Sports
		38	Letters to the Editor

Directions: After reading about tables of contents in magazines, answer these questions about Kids' Life magazine.
1. What page does the story about summer camp begin on?   **Page 12**
2. What page does the sports department begin on?   **Page 36**
3. List the titles of the departments in this magazine:
   1) **Your Health**   2) **Sports**   3) **Letters to the Editor**
4. Can you tell what the Battle of Gettysburg was by reading the table of contents? **Yes** What was it? **A battle in the Civil War.**
5. Is there any information in this magazine about roller skating? **Not unless it's under the Sports heading**

21

Locating Information

The table of contents, located in the fronts of books or magazines, tells a lot about what's inside.

Tables of contents in books list the headings and page numbers for each chapter. Chapters are the parts into which books are divided. Also listed are chapter numbers, the sections and subsections, if any. Look at the sample table of contents below:

Contents:

1. Planting a garden	2
Location	4
Fences	5
2. Seeds	8
Vegetables	
Potatoes	9
Beans	10
Tomatoes	11
Fruit	
Melons	13
Pumpkins	14
3. Caring for a garden	15
Weeding	16
Fertilizing	19

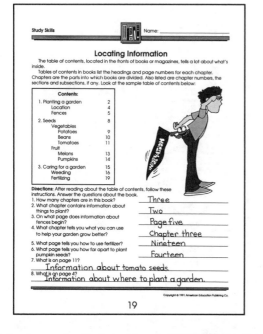

Directions: After reading the table of contents, follow these instructions. Answer the questions about the book.
1. How many chapters are in this book?   **Three**
2. What chapter contains information about things to plant?   **Two**
3. On what page does information about fences begin?   **Page five**
4. What chapter tells you what you can use to help your garden grow better?   **Chapter three**
5. What page tells you how to use fertilizer?   **Nineteen**
6. What page tells you how far apart to plant pumpkin seeds?   **Fourteen**
7. What is on page 11?   **Information about tomato seeds.**
8. What is on page 4?   **Information about where to plant a garden.**

19

Locating Information

LIVING

Table of Contents

EXERCISE Ride for a while with these experienced cyclists. 13
DISCOVERIES Walk with a man through the ditches where he discovered dinosaur bones. 27
HAPPENINGS Earth Day becomes important once again. 5
SCIENCE Find out why astronauts like their jobs. 45
MUSIC Tunes that they sing in the mountains. 33
PEOPLE Read about Dan Quayle and how he got to be vice president. 20
    Talk to Jim Henson, the man behind the muppets. 28
SPORTS Why the Cleveland Indians won't win the title. 42
HISTORY A look at the lives of soldiers who were at Valley Forge. 39

DEPARTMENTS
Living Well 6   Letters to the Editor 9
Comedy 12   Books 16
Movies 24   Snacks 36

Directions: Look at the table of contents above for Living magazine. The articles in it are grouped according to subjects.
1. How many departments are in this issue of the magazine?   **Six**
2. Circle the topics that are regular features in "Living."

(Books)   Dinosaurs   Cleveland Indians   Dan Quayle
(Comedy) (Living Well) (Snacks)   Earth Day

3. Is this Table of contents arranged alphabetically, in the order that articles appear, or by subjects?   **Subjects**
4. What page would you look at if you wanted to see what was playing at movie theaters?   **24**
5. Is there any information in this magazine about football?   **No**
6. Who are the two people featured in this issue?   **Dan Quayle and Jim Henson**
7. Is there anything in this issue about cycling?   **Yes**
8. Under what heading is it listed?   **Exercise**

22

Locating Information

An index is an alphabetical listing of names, topics and important words found in the back of a book. An index lists every page on which these items appear. For example, in a book about music, dulcimer might be listed this way: dulcimer 2, 13, 26, 38. Page numbers may also be listed like this: guitars 18-21. That means that information about guitars begins on page 18 and continues through page 21. Other words to know about indexes include:

subject — the name of the item on an index
sub-entry — a smaller division of the subject. For example, "apples" would be listed under "fruit."

N		*See also planet names.*	
Neptune,	27	Pleiades	32
NGC 5128 (galaxy),	39	Pluto,	12, 27
Novas,	32	Polaris	35, 36
		Pole star. *See Polaris.*	
O		Project Ozma,	41
Observatories. *See El Caracol.*			
Orbital of planets,	10	**R**	
Orion rockets,	43	Rings. *See Planet rings.*	
P		**S**	
Planetoids. *See Asteroids.*		Sagittarius,	37
Planet rings		Satellites	
Jupiter,	23	Jupiter,	24
Saturn,	9, 25	Neptune,	27
Uranus,	26	Pluto,	27
Planets		Saturn,	25
discovered by Greeks,	7	Uranus,	26
outside the solar system,	40	*See also Galilean satellites*	
visible with naked eye,	9	Saturn,	25

Directions: Look at part of the index from a book about the solar system. Then answer the questions.
1. On what pages is there information about Pluto? *Pages 12, 27*
2. On what page is information about Saturn's ring first found? *Page 9*
3. What is on page 41? *Information on project Ozma.*
4. Where is there information about the pole star? *Under Polaris, pages 35-36*
5. What is on page 43? *Information about the Orion Rocket.*
6. On what page would you find information about planets that are visible to the eye? *Page 9*
7. On what page would you find information about Jupiter's satellites? *Page 24*

Review

FARMING
Table of Contents

9	**Farmers of the Midwest** Read about small farmers still trying to survive in the business.
15	**Farmers' Markets** Some farmers take their goods to town and sell them to the city folk.
26	**Hay: The Cheapest Way** New technology helps produce bales of hay quicker and cheaper than in the past.
36	**The Farm Family** Farming is a way of life and everybody helps!
	Departments
	Letters to the Editor 5
	Finances 7
	High Tech 13
	Haymaker 27

INDEX

Africa 6
Alabama 49
Alps 21, 25
Antarctica 10-12
Antarctic Circle 8-10
Arctic 12-14
Arctic Circle 14
Arctic Ocean 15
Asia 37
Athens 33
Atlantic Ocean 11

Baltic Sea 15, 30
Baltimore 51
Black Sea 37
Bombay 39
Brazil 59
British Isles 19
Buffalo 52
Bug River 31

Cadiz 27
California 48
Cambridge 19
Cape of Good Hope 49
China 11, 41
Colorado River, Argentina 61
Colorado River, U.S.A. 62
Continents 2-3
Cuba 55

Directions: Look at the table of contents from "Farming" magazine. Then answer the questions.
1. Is there any information about fashion in this magazine? *No*
2. Is there any information about computers? *Perhaps in the high tech column*
3. Information about children on farms is probably included in which feature? *The family farm*
4. Are there any features about animals in this magazine? *No*

Now look at the index below from a book about the world. Then answer the questions.
1. On what pages would you find information about the Baltic Sea? *15, 30*
2. What is listed on pages 2-3? *Continents*
3. Where are the two Colorado Rivers? *Argentina and the United States.*

Locating Information

Look at the index from a book about music. The letters A, B, C, D, E, F and G after some of the page numbers refer to the names of the units in which the pages are located. Each unit starts with page number one.

Unit A is Listening to Music.
Unit C is Instruments and Orchestras.
Unit E is The Story of Music.
Unit G is Writing Music.

Unit B is Music Around the World.
Unit D is Singing and Dancing.
Unit F is Composers and Their Music.

Index

b
Bach, C.P.E. F3
Bach, J.C. F3
Bach, J.S. A14, B28, D6, E19, F2-3, F7, G12, G13
backing A12, C27
background music B3, see incidental music
bagpipes B30-1
ballad E21
Ballade A12, F8
ballet D26-32, E30
bands B13, B22-3, B30-2
baritone (brass instrument) C10
baritone voice D7
Baroque music D10, D18, D20, E16-17
Bartok F4, F24
bass voice D4, D7
bassoon B31, C4, C6, C24

beating time C79
Beatles A15, A25, B28, C27
Bedford F32
Beethoven A16, B6, B14, E20, E24, F5, F7, F11, G3, G8-9, G13-14
Berlioz E24, F6
Bizet D12
Borodin F24
Brahms A12, A16, E26, F17, F25, G13
brass bands B32
brass instruments B23, C7-10, C24
Britten A9, D12, F28, G13
Bronze Age E5
bugle C10
buskers B17
Byrd E12

Directions: Answer the questions about the index.
1. On what page is there information about beating time? *C29*
2. What subject is mentioned on pages A15, A25, B28 and C27? *The Beatles*
3. On what page is there information about brass bands? *B32*
4. What other entry includes the word "brass"? *Brass instruments*
5. Where else is there information about background music? *Under incidental music*
6. On what page is there information about bugles? *C10*
7. List all pages that mention Beethoven. *A16, B6, B14, E20, E24, F5, F11, G3, G8-9, G13-14*
8. What instrument is discussed on pages B30 and B31? *Bagpipes*

Using Newspapers For Research

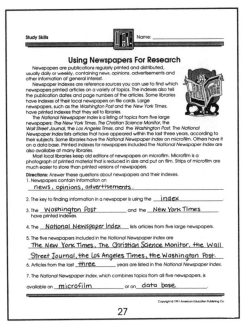

Newspapers are publications regularly printed and distributed, usually daily or weekly, containing news, opinions, advertisements and other information of general interest.

Newspaper indexes are reference sources you can use to find which newspapers printed articles on a variety of topics. The indexes also tell the publication dates and page numbers of the articles. Some libraries have indexes of their local newspapers on file cards. Large newspapers, such as the *Washington Post* and the *New York Times*, have printed indexes that they sell to libraries.

The *National Newspaper Index* is a listing of topics from five large newspapers: *The New York Times*, *The Christian Science Monitor*, the *Wall Street Journal*, the *Los Angeles Times*, and the *Washington Post*. The *National Newspaper Index* lists articles that have appeared within the last three years, according to their subjects. Some libraries have the *National Newspaper Index* on microfilm. Others have it on a data base. Printed indexes for newspapers included the *National Newspaper Index* are also available at many libraries.

Most local libraries keep old editions of newspapers on microfilm. Microfilm is a photograph of printed material that is reduced in size and put on film. Strips of microfilm are much easier to store than printed versions of newspapers.

Directions: Answer these questions about newspapers and their indexes.
1. Newspapers contain information on *news, opinions, advertisements.*
2. The key to finding information in a newspaper is using the *index*
3. The *Washington Post* and the *New York Times* have printed indexes.
4. The *National Newspaper Index* lists articles from five large newspapers.
5. The five newspapers included in the *National Newspaper Index* are *The New York Times, The Christian Science Monitor, the Wall Street Journal, the Los Angeles Times, the Washington Post.*
6. Articles from the last *three* years are listed in the *National Newspaper Index.*
7. The *National Newspaper Index*, which combines topics from all five newspapers, is available on *microfilm* or on *data base*

Locating Information

APPETIZERS
Bacon-wrapped Halibut 92
Scallops with Sorrel and Tomato 116
Shrimp and Basil Beignets 116
Shrimp and Vegetable Spring Rolls with Hoisin and Mustard Sauces 85
Sweet Potato Ribbon Chips 136

SOUPS
Lemongrass Soup, Hot, with Radishes and Chives 84
Roasted Garlic Soup 22
Vegetable Soup with Creamy Asparagus Flan 154

SALADS, SALAD DRESSINGS
Arugula Salad with Roasted Beets, Walnuts and Daikon 158
Chicken, Fennel, Orange and Olive Salad 24
Jicama Salad 81
Tomato, Onion and Zucchini Salad 152
Walnut Vinaigrette 55

Directions: Some magazines are beginning to use simple indexes to guide their readers to information that they contain. Look at the segment of an index in *Bon Appétit* magazine. Then answer the questions.
1. How many kinds of salads are listed in this issue? *4*
2. What is the recipe that contains radishes? *Lemongrass soup*
3. Name the recipe found on page 24. *Chicken, Fennel, Orange and Olive salad.*
4. On what page would you find an appetizer that includes scallops? *Page 116*
   What is the name of that recipe? *Scallops with Sorrel and Tomato*
5. Can you find any listings that contain halibut, a kind of fish? *Yes, Bacon wrapped Halibut.*
6. On what page is there a recipe made from sweet potatoes? *Page 136*
   What is the name of the recipe? *Sweet Potato ribbon chips*
   For what part of a meal would it be served? *As an appetizer*

Using Newspapers For Research

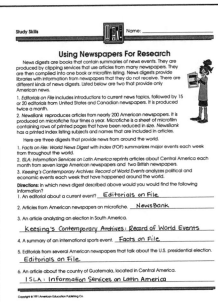

News digests are books that contain summaries of news events. They are produced by clipping services that use articles from many newspapers. They are then compiled into one book or microfilm listing. News digests provide libraries with information from newspapers that they do not receive. There are different kinds of news digests. Listed below are two that provide only American news.

1. *Editorials on File* includes introductions to current news topics, followed by 15 or 20 editorials from United States and Canadian newspapers. It is produced twice a month.
2. *NewsBank* reproduces articles from nearly 200 American newspapers. It is produced on microfiche twice a year. Microfiche is a sheet of microfilm containing rows of printed pages that have been reduced in size. *NewsBank* has a printed index listing subjects and names that are included in articles.

Here are three digests that provide news from around the world.

1. *Facts on File: World News Digest with Index* (FOF) summarizes major events each week from throughout the world.
2. *ISLA: Information Services on Latin America* reprints articles about Central America each month from seven large American newspapers and two British newspapers.
3. *Keesing's Contemporary Archives: Record of World Events* analyzes political and economic events each week that have happened around the world.

Directions: In which news digest described above would you would find the following information?
1. An editorial about a current event? *Editorials on File*
2. Articles from American newspapers on microfiche. *NewsBank*
3. An article analyzing an election in South America. *Keesing's Contemporary Archives: Record of World Events*
4. A summary of an international sports event. *Facts on File*
5. Editorials from several American newspapers that talk about the U.S. presidential election. *Editorials on File*
6. An article about the country of Guatemala, located in Central America. *ISLA: Information Services on Latin America*

Study Skills Name: ____________

Using Newspapers For Research

Some news digests contain information from foreign newspapers that have been translated into English. These digests provide information about events in other countries.

1. *African Recorder: a Fortnightly Record of African Events* includes articles from African and Asian newspapers, magazines, radio broadcasts and government sources published each week.
2. *Asian Recorder: Weekly Digest of Asian Events* is similar to the *African Recorder* and gathers much of its news from the same sources each week.
3. *Canadian News Facts: The Indexed Digest of Canadian Current Events (CNF)* summarizes articles from 20 leading Canadian newspapers and several news agencies. It is published every two weeks.
4. *Current Digest of the Soviet Press (CDSP)* translates some articles from Soviet magazines and newspapers (such as Pravda) into the English language each week.
5. *Foreign Broadcast Information Service (FBIS)* reports news each day about China, Central America, Eastern Europe and the Soviet Union taken from television broadcasts, newspapers, press agencies and governement statements.

Directions: Answer these questions about how to get information from other countries.

1. The African Recorder and the Asian Recorder gather news from African and Asian newspapers, magazines, radio broadcasts and government sources.
2. Translations of Russian articles can be found in the Current Digest of the Soviet Press.
3. The *Foreign Broadcast Information Service* reprints news from sources in China, Central America, Eastern Europe and the Soviet Union.
4. Summaries of articles taken from 20 Canadian newspapers are included in Canadian News Facts
5. Articles from *Pravda* can be found in the Current Digest of the Soviet Press.
6. The only daily report listed above is the Foreign Broadcast Information Service.
7. Summaries of articles about Canada's schools can be found in Canadian News Facts.

Copyright © 1991 American Education Publishing Co.

Study Skills Name: ____________

Using Newspapers For Research

Articles from old newspapers are on file in some libraries. The *Great Contemporary Issues Series* is a group of books that contains articles. Some reprinted from the *New York Times* are from as far back as the 1860s. More than 30 books are in the series, ranging in topics from big business to China to medicine to health care. Here are the names of other collections of newspapers that also can be found in some local libraries.

1. *Canadian Newspapers on Microfilm* has more than 300 Canadian newspapers from the 1800s and 1900s.
2. *Civil War Newspapers on Microfilm* includes more than 300 articles from newspapers printed during the Civil War, from 1861 to 1865.
3. *Contemporary Newspapers of the North American Indian* includes 49 newspapers from several states during 1960s and 1970s.
4. *Early American Newspapers* includes copies of some of the newspapers listed in the book *History and Bibliography of American Newspapers, 1690-1820.*
5. *Negro Newspapers on Microfilm* includes parts and entire copies of nearly 200 black American newspapers published from the mid-1800s to the mid-1900s.
6. *The Newspapers of Ireland* includes 25 newspapers from that country published in the 1800s and early 1900s.

Directions: Answer these questions about old newspapers.

1. Newspapers from the Civil War era can be found in Civil War Newspapers on Microfilm.
2. *Early American Newspapers* contains copies of papers published from 1690 to 1820.
3. Old newspapers from Ireland can be found in The Newspapers of Ireland.
4. Copies of newspapers that are listed in *History and Bibliography of American Newspapers, 1690-1820* can be found in Early American Newspapers.
5. One of the best places to find information about slavery during the American Civil War would be Negro Newspapers on Microfilm.
6. Information about Indians in 1971 could be found by looking in the Contemporary Newspapers of the North American Indian.
7. Information about early elections in Canada could be found in Canadian Newspapers on Microfilm.

Copyright © 1991 American Education Publishing Co.

Study Skills Name: ____________

Using Newspapers For Research

When libraries borrow books, magazines or newspapers from other libraries it is called interlibrary loan. To find out which libraries have certain newspapers, use one of these two sources: *Newspapers in Microform: U.S., 1948-72* or *Newspapers in Microform: Foreign Countries, 1948-72.*

The *American Library Directory* provides addresses of libraries throughout the country. Look at this listing from the *American Library Directory*. All of these libraries are in Massachusetts. Their towns are listed in bold at the top of each entry.

CLARKSBURG — 1871. Area code 413

P NORTH ADAMS PUBLIC LIBRARY, Church St, North Adams, 01247. SAN 307-3327. Tel 413-662-2545. *Librn* Lisa Jarisch
Founded 1884. Pop served 16,000; Circ 60,000
1988-89 Income $163,444. Exp $28,415, Bks $23,500, Per $3500, Other Print Mat $65, Micro $225, AV Mats $1125; Sal $111,000
Library Holdings: Bk vols 40,000; Per sub 120
Mem of Western Regional Pub Libr Syst

CLINTON — 12,771. Area code 508

P BIGELOW FREE PUBLIC LIBRARY, 54 Walnut St, 01510. SAN 307-3335. Tel 508-365-5052; Interlibrary Loan Service Tel. No.: 799-1683. *Librn* Christine Flaherty
Pop served 12,891; Circ 40,981
1987-88 Income $104,330. Exp Bks $18,600, Per $3000, AV Mats $500; Sal $74,182
Library Holdings: Bk vols 105,000
Mem of Cent Mass Regional Libr Syst

COLRAIN — 1552. Area code 413

P GRISWOLD MEMORIAL LIBRARY, Main St, 01340. SAN 307-
Founded 1908. Pop served 1493

Directions: Use the information above to answer the following questions.

1. What is it called when libraries borrow newspapers and other materials from other libraries? Interlibrary loan
2. To find a newspaper printed in the United States in 1968, where would you look? Newspapers in Microform : U.S., 1948-72
3. How would you locate a German newspaper from 1950? Newspapers in Microform : Foreign Countries, 1948-72
4. Addresses for libraries throughout the country can be found in the American Library Directory.
5. In the listing from the *American Library Directory*, "Lbrn" is the abbreviation for librarian. Who is the librarian at the North Adams Public Library? Lisa Jarisch

Copyright © 1991 American Education Publishing Co.

Study Skills Name: ____________

Using Newspapers For Research

Although some newspapers are no longer published, libraries still may have information about them. The *History and Bibliography of American Newspapers, 1690-1820* is a reference book that documents newspapers from throughout those years. Another book, *American Newspapers, 1821-1936*, lists more newspapers. Newspapers that are published today are listed in the *Gale Directory of Publications and Broadcast Media.*

Look at this listing for the *Tule River Times* taken from the *Gale Directory*. The number, 3695, is the listing number for that newspaper.

SPRINGVILLE

Print

3695 Tule River Times
P.O. Box 692
Springville, CA 93265 Phone: (209) 539-3166
Community newspaper. **Estab.:** August 1979. **Frequency:** Weekly.
Printing Method: Offset. **Trim Size:** 11 1/4x14. Cols./Page: 5.
Col Width: 11 picas. **Col. Depth:** 13 in. **Key Personnel:** Pamela Holve, Managing Editor and Co-Publisher.
Subscription: $15.00.
Ad Rate: BW: $185.25 **Circulation:** Paid +1,000
PCI: $3.15 Free +12
Color advertising not accepted.

Directions: Answer these questions about newspaper directories.

1. What publication would list newspapers printed in 1790? History and Bibliography of American Newspapers, 1690-1820
2. Where would a newspaper printed in 1889 be listed? American Newspapers, 1821-1936
3. To find newspapers published in California today, where would you look? Gale Directory of Publications and Broadcast Media
4. How often is the *Tule River Times* published? Weekly
5. Does the *Gale Directory* list the page size of the *Tule River Times*? (Tip: Look for the words "Trim Size.") Yes
6. When was the *Tule River Times* established? August 1979
7. What is the telephone number of the *Tule River Times*? (209) 539-3166
8. What is the cost of a subscription to the *Tule River Times*? $15

Copyright © 1991 American Education Publishing Co.

Study Skills Name: ____________

Using Newspapers For Research

Directions: Choose one of the newspaper projects listed below and complete it at your local library. Use this page for notes.

1. Use the *National Newspaper Index* to find articles about ice hockey player Wayne Gretzky. On a separate piece of paper, list five of these articles and the newspapers in which they appeared. Find one of the articles in the microfilm files at the library. Summarize the article after you have read it.
2. Use *Editorials on File* at the library to find 10 of the current editorial topics addressed by newspapers. List the topics on a separate sheet of paper. Do any of them address education or health issues? Read several editorial summaries on those or other subjects in the booklet and write a brief report about them.
3. Use *Facts on File: World News Digest with Index* to find summaries of any articles related to the space exploration program in the Soviet Union. Write a brief report about these summaries.
4. Use the latest issue of the *Current Digest of the Soviet Press* to find articles about Russian teenagers. Use that information to write a story about them.

Answers vary.

Copyright © 1991 American Education Publishing Co.

Study Skills Name: ____________

Review

Directions: Read each question. Then choose one of the news digests listed in the box to answer it.

News Digests:
The New York Times Index
The National Newspaper Index
Editorials on File
NewsBank
African Recorder
Asian Recorder
ISLA: Information Services on Latin America
Current Digest of the Soviet Press
Foreign Broadcast Information Service
Great Contemporary Issue Series
Civil War Newspapers on Microfilm
Contemporary Newspapers of the North American Indian
Early American Newspapers, 1704-1820
Negro Newspapers on Microfilm
Newspapers in Microform: U.S.
Newspapers in Microform: Foreign Countries
Gale Directory

1. Which publication includes American newspapers published from 1704-1820? Early American Newspapers
2. Where are newspapers of today listed? Gale Directory
3. Which publication includes summaries of editorials written in several newspapers? Editorials on File
4. Where would articles about Soviet school reform be found? Current Digest of the Soviet Press
5. Name the series of books that includes articles from the *New York Times* dating back to 1860? Great Contemporary Issue Series
6. Where would an article about slavery in the mid-1800s be reproduced? Negro Newspapers on Microfilm
7. Name five publications that include articles from foreign newspapers:

1) African Recorder 2) Asian Recorder
3) Canadian News Facts 4) Current Digest of the Soviet Press
5) Foreign Broadcast Information Service

Copyright © 1991 American Education Publishing Co.

Doing Biographical Research

A biography is a written history of a person's life. Often information for a biography can be obtained from an encyclopedia, especially if a person is famous. Of course, not everyone is listed in a main article in an encyclopedia. Use the encyclopedia's index, which is the last book in the set, to find which volume contains the information you need. Look at this listing taken from an encyclopedia index for Henry Moore, an English artist:

MOORE, HENRY English sculptor, 1898-1986
main article Moore 12:106b, illus.
references in Sculpture 15:290a, illus.

LINCOLN, ABRAHAM president of US, 1809-65	operatic soprano admired for vocal purity
main article Lincoln 11:49a, illus.	and control; made debut 1838 in Stockholm
references in	and sang in Paris and London becoming known
Assassination 2:64b	as the "Swedish Nightingale"; toured US with
Caricature: illus. 4:87	P.T. Barnum1850; last concert 1883
Civil War, American 4:296a fol.	*references in* Barnum 2:235a
Confederate States of America 5:113b fol.	LINDBERGH, ANNE US aviator, b. 1907
Democracy 6:17a	*references in* Lindbergh 11:53b, illus.
Gettysburg, Battle of 8:144a	LINDBERGH, CHARLES AUGUSTUS US
Illinois 9:259b	aviator, 1902-74
Thanksgiving Day 17:199a	*main article* Lindbergh 11:53a, illus.
United States of America, history of 18:137a fol.	*references in*
Westward Movement 19:49a	Aviation, history of 2:140b, illus.
LINCOLN, BENJAMIN US army officer,	Medals and decorations 11:266b
1733-1810	Saint Louis 15:215b
references in American Revolution 1:204b	LINDE, KARL VON German engineer,
LIND, JENNY Swedish singer, 1820-87;	1842-1934
	references in Refrigeration 15:32b

Notice that the listing includes Henry Moore's dates of birth and death. It also includes a short description of his accomplishments: he was an English sculptor. Look below at part of the index from the *Children's Britannica* encyclopedias. Then answer the questions.

Directions: Answer these questions about biographical research.

1. Where is the main article for Abraham Lincoln?
11.49a (Volume 11, page 49, the left column (a))

2. In addition to the main article, how many other places are there references to Abraham Lincoln? 10

3. In which encyclopedia volume is there information about Anne Lindbergh? 11

4. What is the title of the main article in which Anne Lindbergh is mentioned? Lindbergh

35 　　Copyright © 1991 American Education Publishing Co.

Doing Biographical Research

Directions: Use biographical dictionaries to research a person listed below. Remember to begin with one or more biographical master indexes. There may be more than one biographical dictionary that contains information about the person. Write a report about that person's life in the space provided. Use additional paper, if necessary.

Ronald Reagan　　　Woody Allen　　　Elizabeth Dole
John Glenn　　　Andrew Lloyd Webber　　　Elizabeth Taylor

Answers vary.

_____

_____

_____

_____

_____

_____

_____

_____

_____

_____

_____

_____

_____

_____

_____

Copyright © 1991 American Education Publishing Co.　　　38

Doing Biographical Research

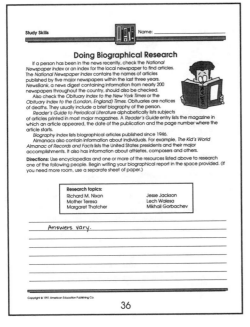

If a person has been in the news recently, check the *National Newspaper Index* or an index for the local newspaper to find articles. The *National Newspaper Index* contains the names of articles published by five major newspapers within the last three years. *NewsBank*, a news digest containing information from nearly 200 newspapers throughout the country, should also be checked.

Also check the *Obituary Index to the New York Times* or the *Obituary Index to the (London, England) Times*. Obituaries are notices of deaths. They usually include a brief biography of the person.

Reader's Guide to Periodical Literature alphabetically lists subjects of articles printed in most major magazines. A *Reader's Guide* entry lists the magazine in which an article appeared, the date of the publication and the page number where the article starts.

Biography Index lists biographical articles published since 1946.

Almanacs also contain information about individuals. For example, *The Kid's World Almanac of Records and Facts* lists the United States presidents and their major accomplishments. It also has information about athletes, composers and others.

Directions: Use encyclopedias and one or more of the resources listed above to research one of the following people. Begin writing your biographical report in the space provided. (If you need more room, use a separate sheet of paper.)

Research topics:	
Richard M. Nixon	Jesse Jackson
Mother Teresa	Lech Walesa
Margaret Thatcher	Mikhail Gorbachev

Answers vary.

_____

_____

_____

_____

_____

_____

_____

Copyright © 1991 American Education Publishing Co.　　　36

Doing Biographical Research

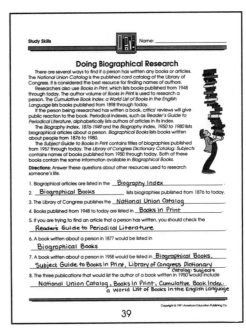

There are several ways to find if a person has written any books or articles. The *National Union Catalog* is the published card catalog of the Library of Congress. It is considered the best resource for finding names of authors.

Researchers also use *Books in Print*, which lists books published from 1948 through today. The author volume of *Books in Print* is used to research a person. The *Cumulative Book Index: a World List of Books in the English Language* lists books published from 1898 through today. If the person being researched has written a book, critics' reviews will give public reaction to the book. Periodical indexes, such as *Reader's Guide to Periodical Literature*, alphabetically lists authors of articles in its index.

The *Biography Index, 1876-1949* and the *Biography Index, 1950 to 1980* lists biographical articles about a person. *Biographical Books* lists books about people from 1876 to 1980.

The *Subject Guide to Books in Print* contains titles of biographies published from 1957 through today. The *Library of Congress Dictionary Catalog: Subjects* contains names of books published from 1950 through today. Both of these books contain the same information available in *Biographical Books*.

Directions: Answer these questions about other resources used to research someone's life.

1. Biographical articles are listed in the Biography Index

2. Biographical Books lists biographies published from 1876 to today.

3. The Library of Congress publishes the National Union Catalog

4. Books published from 1948 to today are listed in Books in Print

5. If you are trying to find an article that a person has written, you should check the Reader's Guide to Periodical Literature

6. A book written about a person in 1877 would be listed in Biographical Books

7. A book written about a person in 1958 would be listed in Biographical Books, Subject Guide to Books in Print, Library of Congress Dictionary Catalog: Subjects

8. The three publications that would list the author of a book written in 1950 would include National Union Catalog, Books in Print, Cumulative Book Index: a World List of Books in the English Language

Copyright © 1991 American Education Publishing Co.　　　39

Doing Biographical Research

Biographical dictionaries, such as *Who's Who*, contain histories of peoples' lives. In addition to *Who's Who*, there are many other biographical dictionaries. BDs, as they are called, can include books such as the *Biographical Dictionary of English Architects* or *Who's Who in Art Materials*. Some biographical dictionaries list only people who lived during certain eras, such as *Women Artists: 1550-1950*.

Because there are so many biographical dictionaries, master indexes are published to guide researchers. Up to 500 books are listed in some biographical master indexes. A master index may list several biographical dictionaries in which information about a person can be obtained.

There are several different biographical master indexes. Here are a few.

1. The *Biography and Genealogy Master Index* contains 11 books and is a good place to begin research. Parts of this index, such as *Children's Authors and Illustrators*, are in separate volumes.

2. *An Analytical Bibliography of Universal Collected Biography* contains information from more than 3,000 biographical dictionaries published before 1933.

3. *In Black and White: A Guide to Magazine Articles, Newspaper Articles and Books Concerning More than 15,000 Black Individuals and Groups* is the title of a large biographical master index.

4. *Marquis Who's Who Publications: Index to All Books* lists names from at least 15 *Who's Who* books published by Marquis each year.

Directions: Complete each sentence about biographical master indexes.

1. Biographical dictionaries contain
information about people's lives.

2. When beginning research in biographical dictionaries, first use a
biographical master index.

3. The _ has 11 books in its set.
Biography and Genealogy Master Index

4. *Children's Authors and Illustrators* is a separate volume of the
Biography and Genealogy Master Index.

5. Information from at least 15 *Who's Who* publications each year is contained in the
Marquis Who's Who Publications: Index to All Books.

6. Information from old biographical dictionaries can be found in
An Analytical Bibliography of Universal Collected Biography.

Copyright © 1991 American Education Publishing Co.　　　37

Doing Biographical Research

Information about people who belong to clubs, trade unions or other organizations can sometimes be found in libraries or from an organization's main office. If these people worked for corporations, information may be obtained by contacting the public relations office of that company.

Unpublished materials, such as diaries or letters, are usually donated to a library or a historical society when a person dies. Clues that such materials exist may be found when reading other books or articles about a person.

Personal interviews can also provide information about subjects. A few points to remember when conducting an interview:

1. Cover the five main points that you need to know for any story: who, what, when, where and why.
2. Write accurate notes while doing the interview.
3. Use the notes to write the article.
4. If your notes are unclear, check them with the person interviewed.
5. Double check other facts that you are not sure about. Be sure to check the spelling of the person's name and check important dates that were mentioned during the interview.
6. Only write things that you are sure the person said.

Directions: After reading about other ways to research a person's life, use the tips listed above to conduct an interview with a friend or classmate. Write a brief biography containing what you learned during the interview.

Answers vary.

_____

_____

_____

_____

_____

_____

_____

_____

_____

Copyright © 1991 American Education Publishing Co.　　　40

Doing Biographical Research

Directions: Look at the names listed below. Choose one of them to research, then write a biographical article on a separate sheet of paper. Put a check beside each listed resource you used. (You may not have to use all of them.)

Subjects:
Judy Blume, author
Dale Murphy, baseball player
Henry J. Heimlich, doctor
Diana Ross, singer
Ted Kennedy, politician

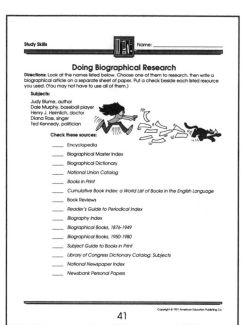

Check these sources:

____ Encyclopedia
____ Biographical Master Index
____ Biographical Dictionary
____ National Union Catalog
____ Books in Print
____ Cumulative Book Index: a World List of Books in the English Language
____ Book Reviews
____ Reader's Guide to Periodical Index
____ Biography Index
____ Biographical Books, 1876-1949
____ Biographical Books, 1950-1980
____ Subject Guide to Books in Print
____ Library of Congress Dictionary Catalog: Subjects
____ National Newspaper Index
____ Newsbank Personal Papers

41

Copyright © 1991 American Education Publishing Co.

Review

Directions: Read each heading and follow the instructions.

A. Write T or F on the line beside each statement.

F 1. Do not use a biographical master index before checking *Who's Who in American Education.*

T 2. A biographical dictionary lists people and their histories.

F 3. The *Biographical Dictionary of English Architects* is a *Biographical Master Index.*

F 4. A biographical master index includes listings from only one biographical dictionary.

B. Choose the correct word from the word box to complete each sentence.

articles	index	contents	atlases	resource	almanacs

1. Before finding a listing in an encyclopedia, you should use the encyclopedia **index** .

2. The *Reader's Guide to Periodical Literature* lists **articles** published in most major magazines.

3. *Biography Index* is a **resource** that lists articles published about people since 1946.

4. **Almanacs** list odd bits of information about people.

C. Write book or article on the line to tell whether the index named would list books or articles.

1. *Biography Index* — **article**

2. *Reader's Guide to Periodical Literature* — **article**

3. *Books in Print* — **book**

4. *National Union Catalog* — **book**

D. Fill in the blanks to complete the sentences.

1. A person's original writings would include his or her diary or **letters** .

2. If a person worked for a corporation, you could gain information about him or her by contacting that firm's **public relations** office.

Copyright © 1991 American Education Publishing Co.

42

Determining The Author's Purpose

Authors write to entertain, inform or persuade. To entertain means to hold the attention of or to amuse the reader. A fiction book about ghosts entertains its reader, as does a joke book.

To inform means to give factual information. A cookbook informs the reader of new recipes. A newspaper tells what is happening in the world.

To persuade means to convince. Newspaper editorial writers try to persuade readers to accept their opinions. Doctors write health columns to persuade readers to eat healthy foods.

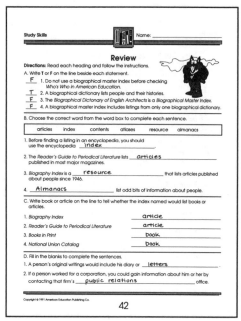

Directions: Look at the passages below. Tell whether they entertain, inform or persuade. (They may do more than one.) Give the reasons why. The first one is done for you.

George Washington was born in a brick house near the Potamac River in Virginia on Feb. 11, 1732. When he was 11 years old, George went to live with his half-brother, Lawrence, at Mount Vernon.

Author's Purpose: To inform

Reason: It gives factual information

When George Washington was a child he always measured and counted things. Maybe that is why he became a surveyor when he grew up. Surveyors like to measure and count things, too.

Author's Purpose: To inform

Reason: It gives factual information

George Washington was the best president Americans ever had. He led a new nation to independence. He made all of the states feel as if they were part of the United States. All presidents are as involved with the country as George Washington.

Author's Purpose: To persuade

Reason: It tries to convince readers that George Washington was the best president

Before George Washington was married, he loved to dance with women at parties. He fell in love many times. Before he met his wife, Martha, he proposed to two other women. They both turned him down. But George Washington was not defeated. Finally, Martha Custis agreed to marry him. They lived a happy life together.

Author's Purpose: To inform or entertain

Reason: It tells about George Washington's private life and it amuses the readers

Copyright © 1991 American Education Publishing Co.

43

Determining The Author's Purpose

Directions: Read each paragraph. Tell whether they inform, entertain or persuade. One paragraph does more than one. Then write your reason on the line below:

A llama (LAW' MAW) is a South American animal that is related to the camel. It is raised for its wool. Also, it can carry heavy loads. Some people who live near mountains in the United States train llamas to go on mountain trips. Llamas are sure-footed because they have two long toes and toenails.

Author's Purpose: To inform

Reason: It gives factual information about llamas

Llama's are the best animals to have if you're planning to back-pack in the mountains. They can climb easily and carry your supplies. No one should ever go for a long hiking trip in the mountains without a llama.

Author's Purpose: To persuade

Reason: It tries to convince readers that mountain back-packers should take llamas with them

Llamas can be stubborn animals. Sometimes they suddenly stop walking for no reason. People have to push them to get them moving again. Stubborn llamas can be frustrating when hiking up a steep mountain.

Author's Purpose: To entertain and to inform

Reason: It amuses the readers to think about a person trying to push a llama up a mountain, but it also informs them that llamas are stubborn

Greg is an 11-year-old boy who raises llamas to climb mountains. One of his llamas is named Dallas. Although there are special saddles for llamas, Greg likes to ride bareback.

Author's Purpose: To inform

Reason: It provides factual information about a boy who raises llamas

Now use a separate sheet of paper to inform readers about llamas.

(Answers vary but should describe of llamas)

Copyright © 1991 American Education Publishing Co.

44

Determining The Author's Purpose

Directions: Read each paragraph. Determine the author's purpose. Is it to inform, entertain or persuade?

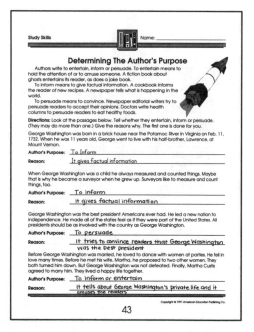

Cookie parties that allow you to sample a variety of cookies can be more fun than pizza parties. The cookies are not hard to bake, but they still taste great. No one should finish the sixth grade without having a cookie party with his or her friends.

Author's Purpose: To persuade

Reason: It tries to convince you to have a cookie party

When planning a cookie party, invite five friends. Ask each of them to bake a half dozen of their favorite cookies. You should also bake six cookies. When they arrive for the party, serve milk and other drinks.

Author's Purpose: To inform

Reason: It explains how to plan a cookie party

Cookie parties can be funny sometimes, too. One girl who went to a cookie party said, "I burnt every cookie that I baked." She brought a package of store-bought cookies with her.

Author's Purpose: To entertain

Reason: It tells a funny story about someone at the party

Make cookie invitations to invite people to your party. Use brown sheets of construction paper and cut them out in round circles so that they look like cookies. Then write your name, your address and the party's date and time on them. Put your telephone number on them, too.

Author's Purpose: To inform

Reason: It explains how to make an invitation

Use a separate sheet of paper to write an entertaining passage about a cookie party.

Answers vary

Copyright © 1991 American Education Publishing Co.

45

Determining The Author's Purpose

Directions: Read each paragraph and determine the author's purpose. Then write your reasons on the line below.

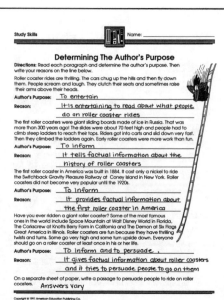

Roller coaster rides are thrilling. The cars chug up the hills and then fly down them. People scream and laugh. They clutch their seats and sometimes raise their arms above their heads.

Author's Purpose: To entertain

Reason: It is entertaining to read about what people do on roller coaster rides

The first roller coasters were giant sliding boards made of ice in Russia. That was more than 300 years ago! The slides were about 70 feet high and people had to climb steep ladders to reach their tops. Riders got into carts and slid down very fast. Then they climbed the ladders again. Early roller coasters were more work than fun.

Author's Purpose: To inform

Reason: It tells factual information about the history of roller coasters

The first roller coaster in America was built in 1884. It cost only a nickel to ride the Switchback Gravity Pleasure Railway at Coney Island in New York. Roller coasters did not become very popular until the 1920s.

Author's Purpose: To inform

Reason: It provides factual information about the first roller coaster in America

Have you ever ridden a giant roller coaster? Some of the most famous ones in the world include Space Mountain at Walt Disney World in Florida, The Corkscrew at Knotts Berry Farm in California and The Demon at Six Flags Great America in Illinois. Roller coasters are fun because they have thrilling twists and turns. Some go very high and some turn upside down. Everyone should go on a roller coaster at least once in his or her life.

Author's Purpose: To inform and to persuade

Reason: It gives factual information about roller coasters and it tries to persuade people to go on them

On a separate sheet of paper, write a passage to persuade people to ride on roller coasters. Answers vary

Copyright © 1991 American Education Publishing Co.

46

Determining The Author's Purpose

Directions: Read each passage about the opera composer Gioacchino Rossini. Then determine the author's purpose.

Gioacchino Rossini was born in Italy in 1792, the son of a town trumpeter and an opera singer. He learned about music and the theater from his parents. Rossini wrote his first opera, which is a drama set to music, when he was 14 years old.

Author's Purpose: To inform

Rossini was particular about the music he liked. "All music is good except the boring kind," he said. His own music was fast-paced and happy-sounding. Writing music came easily to Rossini. He once said, "Give me a laundry list, and I'll set it to music."

Author's Purpose: To inform and to entertain

The Barber of Seville was Rossini's most famous opera. It is still performed today. Rossini signed a contract to write *The Barber of Seville* the day after Christmas in 1815. He spent the next 13 days writing the opera, taking little time to eat. Rossini didn't shave during those 13 days, either. Some people said it was unusual that an opera about a barber would cause Rossini not to shave.

Author's Purpose: To inform and to entertain

Music is usually what people like about operas. Those who enjoy listening to music and watching plays will like operas. If you have never been to an opera, you should go.

Author's Purpose: To persuade

Use the information about operas to write a passage that both informs and entertains. Use a separate sheet of paper.

    Answers vary.

Determining The Author's Purpose

Directions: Read each paragraph about a snack you can make. Then tell the author's purpose.

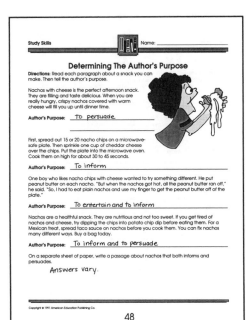

Nachos with cheese are the perfect afternoon snack. They are filling and taste delicious. When you are really hungry, crispy nachos covered with warm cheese will fill you up until dinner time.

Author's Purpose: To persuade

First, spread out 15 or 20 nacho chips on a microwave-safe plate. Then sprinkle one cup of cheddar cheese over the chips. Put the plate into the microwave oven. Cook them on high for about 30 to 45 seconds.

Author's Purpose: To inform

One boy who likes nacho chips with cheese wanted to try something different. He put peanut butter on each nacho. "But when the nachos got hot, all the peanut butter ran off," he said. "So, I had to eat plain nachos and use my finger to get the peanut butter off of the plate."

Author's Purpose: To entertain and to inform

Nachos are a healthful snack. They are nutritious and not too sweet. If you get tired of nachos and cheese, try dipping the chips into potato chip dip before eating them. For a Mexican treat, spread taco sauce on nachos before you cook them. You can fix nachos many different ways. Buy a bag today.

Author's Purpose: To inform and to persuade

On a separate sheet of paper, write a passage about nachos that both informs and persuades.

    Answers vary.

Determining The Author's Purpose

Directions: Read each paragraph. Then identify the author's purpose.

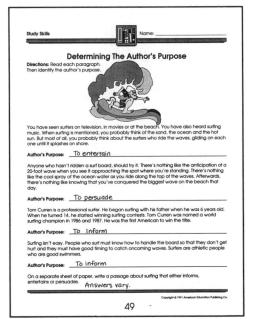

You have seen surfers on television, in movies or at the beach. You have also heard surfing music. When surfing is mentioned, you probably think of the sand, the ocean and the hot sun. But most of all, you probably think about the surfers who ride the waves, gliding on each one until it splashes on shore.

Author's Purpose: To entertain

Anyone who hasn't ridden a surf board, should try it. There's nothing like the anticipation of a 20-foot wave when you see it approaching the spot where you're standing. There's nothing like the cool spray of the ocean water as you ride along the top of the waves. Afterwards, there's nothing like knowing that you've conquered the biggest wave on the beach that day.

Author's Purpose: To persuade

Tom Curren is a professional surfer. He began surfing with his father when he was 6 years old. When he turned 14, he started winning surfing contests. Tom Curren was named a world surfing champion in 1986 and 1987. He was the first American to win the title.

Author's Purpose: To inform

Surfing isn't easy. People who surf must know how to handle the board so that they don't get hurt and they must have good timing to catch oncoming waves. Surfers are athletic people who are good swimmers.

Author's Purpose: To inform

On a separate sheet of paper, write a passage about surfing that either informs, entertains or persuades.

    Answers vary.

Review

Directions: Read each passage about rattlesnakes. Then determine the author's purpose.

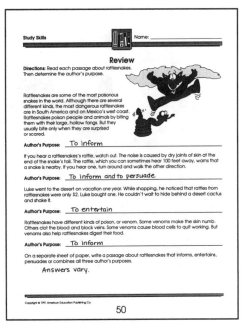

Rattlesnakes are some of the most poisonous snakes in the world. Although there are several different kinds, the most dangerous rattlesnakes are in South America and on Mexico's west coast. Rattlesnakes poison people and animals by biting them with their large, hollow fangs. But they usually bite only when they are surprised or scared.

Author's Purpose: To inform

If you hear a rattlesnake's rattle, watch out. The noise is caused by dry joints of skin at the end of the snake's tail. The rattle, which you can sometimes hear 100 feet away, warns that a snake is nearby. If you hear one, turn around and walk the other direction.

Author's Purpose: To inform and to persuade

Luke went to the desert on vacation one year. While shopping, he noticed that rattles from rattlesnakes were only $2. Luke bought one. He couldn't wait to hide behind a desert cactus and shake it.

Author's Purpose: To entertain

Rattlesnakes have different kinds of poison, or venom. Some venoms make the skin numb. Others clot the blood and block veins. Some venoms cause blood cells to quit working. But venoms also help rattlesnakes digest their food.

Author's Purpose: To inform

On a separate sheet of paper, write a passage about rattlesnakes that informs, entertains, persuades or combines all three author's purposes.

    Answers vary.

Fact Or Opinion?

A fact is something that can be proved. An opinion is a belief not necessarily based on facts.

Dolphins

(1) Dolphins are mammals. (2) They have teeth, they breathe air and they are warm-blooded. (3) They can also grow to be up to 10 feet long. (4) I think that dolphins like people because sometimes they play around ships. (5) But they probably like other dolphins better. (6) They always swim in groups with up to 100 others. (7) Scientists have discovered that dolphins communicate with each other by making different sounds. (8) That is amazing! (9) I think that they probably say a lot of interesting things to each other. (10) Dolphins are now being studied to find out how they "talk" underwater.

Directions: After reading the numbered sentences about dolphins, write in the corresponding numbered blanks whether each sentence gives a fact or an opinion.

1. fact
2. fact
3. fact
4. opinion
5. opinion
6. fact
7. fact
8. opinion
9. opinion
10. fact

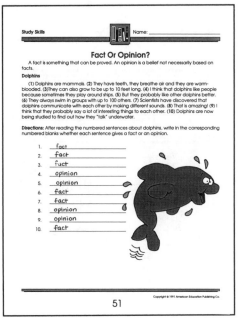

Fact Or Opinion?

Jaws, the Movie

(1) In 1975 a movie was made about a shark that attacked people. (2) It was called *Jaws*. (3) Since then there have been four sequels. (4) I think the first movie was the best one ever made.

(5) The movie featured three main characters: The sheriff, who was afraid to allow people to swim in the ocean; the scientist, who came to town to study the huge creature; and a fisherman, who volunteered to kill the shark. (6) All three of these men were very good actors.

(7) I think the first *Jaws* movie was definitely the scariest. (8) It showed how the people of the town were afraid to swim because of the shark. (9) It showed the three men out on the boat trying to capture the beast. (10) Many people who saw the movie more than once said it was the best movie produced that summer.

Directions: After reading the numbered sentences about a movie called *Jaws*, write in the corresponding blanks whether each sentence gives a fact or an opinion.

1. fact
2. fact
3. fact
4. opinion
5. fact
6. opinion
7. opinion
8. fact
9. fact
10. fact

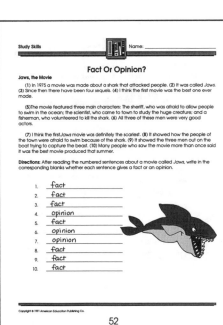

Telling Fact From Opinion

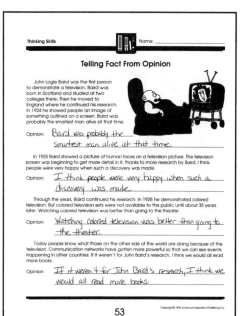

John Logie Baird was the first person to demonstrate a television. Baird was born in Scotland and studied at two colleges there. Then he moved to England where he continued his research. In 1924 he showed people an image of something outlined on a screen. Baird was probably the smartest man alive at that time.

Opinion: *Baird was probably the smartest man alive at that time.*

In 1925 Baird showed a picture of human faces on a television picture. The television screen was beginning to get more detail in it, thanks to more research by Baird. I think people were very happy when such a discovery was made.

Opinion: *I think people were very happy when such a discovery was made.*

Through the years, Baird continued his research. In 1928 he demonstrated colored television. But colored television sets were not available to the public until about 35 years later. Watching colored television was better than going to the theater.

Opinion: *Watching colored television was better than going to the theater.*

Today people know what those on the other side of the world are doing because of the television. Communication networks have gotten more powerful so that we can see events happening in other countries. If it weren't for John Baird's research, I think we would all read more books.

Opinion: *If it weren't for John Baird's research, I think we would all read more books.*

Fact Or Opinion?

Carol's Country Restaurant

(1) I have visited Carol's Country Restaurant seven times in the past two weeks. (2) The meals there are excellent. (3) They often feature country dishes such as meatloaf, ham and scalloped potatoes and fried chicken.

(4) Owner Carol Murphy makes wonderful vegetable soup that includes all home-grown vegetables. (5) It's simmered with thin egg noodles. (6) Another of my favorite dishes is Carol's chili. (7) I'm sure it is the spiciest chili this side of the Mississippi River. (8) Carol says she uses secret ingredients in all of her dishes.

(9) Whether ordering a main dish or a dessert, you can't go wrong at Carol's. (10) Everything is superb.

(11) Carol's Country Restaurant is on Twig Street in Freeport. (12) Prices for main entrees range from $2.50 to $5.95.

Directions: After reading the numbered sentences about Carol's Country Restaurant, write in the corresponding numbered blanks whether each sentence gives a fact or an opinion.

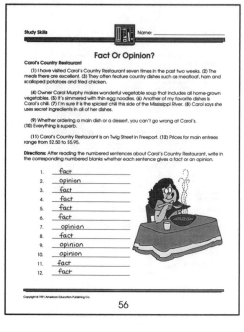

1. fact
2. opinion
3. fact
4. fact
5. fact
6. fact
7. opinion
8. fact
9. opinion
10. opinion
11. fact
12. fact

Fact Or Opinion?

Movie Maker Videos

(1) We think you should visit Movie Maker Videos today. (2) We carry the largest selection of movies in the city. (3) Our shelves are loaded with the best comedies, dramas and adventure films on earth! (4) We think Movie Maker Videos is the best store in town.

(5) We alphabetize all our movies, according to their titles. (6) You won't have to spend hours looking for flicks. (7) Use our handy computer system to learn if a movie has been checked out. (8) You'll like us so much that you won't want to go anywhere else.

(9) At Movie Maker Videos we stock 2,000 films. (10) You will be happy you came to see us first. (11) We charge only $3.50 a night to rent a movie. (12) Visit Movie Maker Videos at 22 Sawville Road in Bloomington.

Directions: After reading the following advertisement for a video rental store, write in the corresponding numbered blank whether each sentence gives a fact or an opinion.

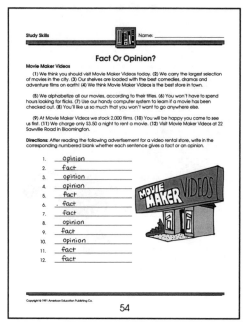

1. opinion
2. fact
3. opinion
4. opinion
5. fact
6. fact
7. fact
8. opinion
9. fact
10. opinion
11. fact
12. fact

Fact Or Opinion?

Thunderbird Jets

(1) The United States Air Force Thunderbirds are a group of red, white and blue jets that do shows for people. (2) The Thunderbirds do special kinds of stunts. (3) Their performances are awesome.

(4) One stunt, called the arrowhead roll, is when four jets form a huge arch in the sky. (5) It is an amazing trick! (6) The planes fly only a few feet apart.

(7) One of the Thunderbird's jets is called the F-16 Fighting Falcon. (8) But through the years there have been many planes that were included in the Thunderbirds. (9) Regardless of what they fly, this Airforce team is delightful.

(10) The Air Force specially trains pilots who fly these jets. (11) Before they can go on the Thunderbird team, the pilots have to have flown a jet fighter for at least 1,000 hours. (12) Being a Thunderbird pilot is the most exciting job on earth!

Directions: After reading the numbered sentences about Thunderbird Jets, write in the corresponding numbered blanks whether each sentence gives a fact or an opinion.

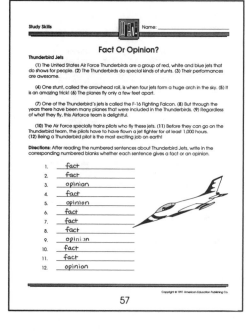

1. fact
2. fact
3. opinion
4. fact
5. opinion
6. fact
7. fact
8. fact
9. opinion
10. fact
11. fact
12. opinion

Fact Or Opinion?

Directions: Read about chilies and peppers. Find the one opinion in each passage.

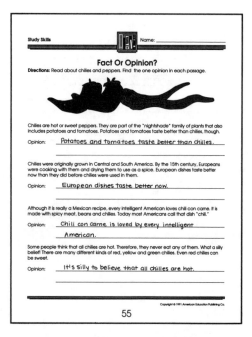

Chilies are hot or sweet peppers. They are part of the "nightshade" family of plants that also includes potatoes and tomatoes. Potatoes and tomatoes taste better than chilies, though.

Opinion: *Potatoes and tomatoes taste better than chilies.*

Chilies were originally grown in Central and South America. By the 15th century, Europeans were cooking with them and drying them to use as a spice. European dishes taste better now than they did before chilies were used in them.

Opinion: *European dishes taste better now.*

Although it is really a Mexican recipe, every intelligent American loves chili con carne. It is made with spicy meat, beans and chilies. Today most Americans call that dish "chili."

Opinion: *Chili con carne is loved by every intelligent American.*

Some people think that all chilies are hot. Therefore, they never eat any of them. What a silly belief! There are many different kinds of red, yellow and green chilies. Even red chilies can be sweet.

Opinion: *It's silly to believe that all chilies are hot.*

Review

The Thunderbirds Fly Again

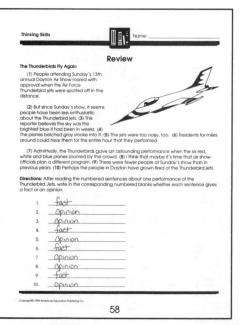

(1) People attending Sunday's 13th annual Dayton Air Show roared with approval when the Air Force Thunderbird jets were spotted off in the distance.

(2) But since Sunday's show, it seems people have been less enthusiastic about the Thunderbird jets. (3) This reporter believes the sky was the brightest blue it had been in weeks. (4) The planes belched gray smoke into it. (5) The jets were too noisy, too. (6) Residents for miles around could hear them for the entire hour that they performed.

(7) Admittedly, the Thunderbirds gave an astounding performance when the six red, white and blue planes zoomed by the crowd. (8) I think that maybe it's time that air show officials use a different program. (9) There were fewer people at Sunday's show than in previous years. (10) Perhaps the people in Dayton have grown tired of the Thunderbird jets.

Directions: After reading the numbered sentences about one performance of the Thunderbird Jets, write in the corresponding numbered blanks whether each sentence gives a fact or an opinion.

1. fact
2. opinion
3. opinion
4. fact
5. opinion
6. fact
7. opinion
8. opinion
9. fact
10. opinion

Page 59

Preparing For And Taking Tests

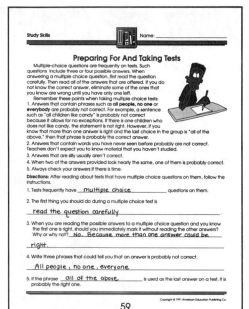

Multiple-choice questions are frequently on tests. Such questions include three or four possible answers. When answering a multiple choice question, first read the question carefully. Then read all of the answers that are offered. If you do not know the correct answer, eliminate some of the ones that you know are wrong until you have only one left.

Remember these points when taking multiple choice tests:
1. Answers that contain phrases such as **all people, no one** or **everybody** are probably not correct. For example, a sentence such as "all children like candy" is probably not correct because it allows for no exceptions. If there is one children who does not like candy, the statement is not right. However, if you know that more than one answer is right and the last choice in the group is "all of the above," then that phrase is probably the correct answer.
2. Answers that contain words you have never seen before probably are not correct. Teachers don't expect you to know material that you haven't studied.
3. Answers that are silly usually aren't correct.
4. When two of the answers provided look nearly the same, one of them is probably correct.
5. Always check your answers if there is time.

Directions: After reading about tests that have multiple choice questions on them, follow the instructions.

1. Tests frequently have ___multiple choice___ questions on them.

2. The first thing you should do during a multiple choice test is
___read the question carefully___

3. When you are reading the possible answers to a multiple choice question and you know the first one is right, should you immediately mark it without reading the other answers? Why or why not? ___No. Because more than one answer could be___
___right.___

4. Write three phrases that could tell you that an answer is probably not correct.
___All people, no one, everyone___

5. If the phrase ___all of the above___ is used as the last answer on a test, it is probably the right one.

Page 60

Preparing For And Taking Tests

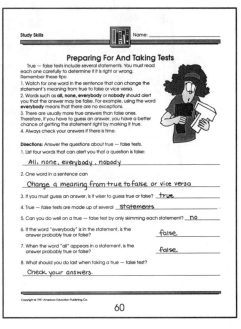

True — false tests include several statements. You must read each one carefully to determine if it is right or wrong. Remember these tips:
1. Watch for one word in the sentence that can change the statement's meaning from true to false or vice versa.
2. Words such as **all, none, everybody** or **nobody** should alert you that the answer may be false. For example, using the word **everybody** means that there are no exceptions.
3. There are usually more true answers than false ones. Therefore, if you have to guess an answer, you have a better chance of getting the statement right by marking it true.
4. Always check your answers if there is time.

Directions: Answer the questions about true — false tests.

1. List four words that can alert you that a question is false:
___All, none, everybody, nobody___

2. One word in a sentence can
___Change a meaning from true to false or vice versa___

3. If you must guess an answer, is it wiser to guess true or false? ___true___

4. True — false tests are made up of several ___statements___

5. Can you do well on a true — false test by only skimming each statement? ___no___

6. If the word "everybody" is in the statement, is the answer probably true or false? ___false___

7. When the word "all" appears in a statement, is the answer probably true or false? ___false___

8. What should you do last when taking a true — false test?
___Check your answers.___

Page 61

Preparing For And Taking Tests

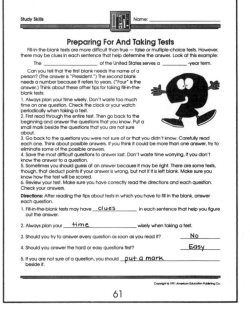

Fill-in-the-blank tests are more difficult than true — false or multiple-choice tests. However, there may be clues in each sentence that help determine the answer. Look at this example:

The _____ of the United States serves a _____ -year term.

Can you tell that the first blank needs the name of a person? (The answer is "President.") The second blank needs a number because it refers to years. ("Four" is the answer.) Think about these other tips for taking fill-in-the-blank tests:
1. Always plan your time wisely. Don't waste too much time on one question. Check the clock or your watch periodically when taking a test.
2. First read through the entire test. Then go back to the beginning and answer the questions that you know. Put a small mark beside the questions that you are not sure about.
3. Go back to the questions you were not sure of or that you didn't know. Carefully read each one. Think about possible answers. If you think it could be more than one answer, try to eliminate some of the possible answers.
4. Save the most difficult questions to answer last. Don't waste time worrying. If you don't know the answer to a question.
5. Sometimes you should guess at an answer because it may be right. There are some tests, though, that deduct points if your answer is wrong, but not if it is left blank. Make sure you know how the test will be scored.
6. Review your test. Make sure you have correctly read the directions and each question. Check your answers.

Directions: After reading the tips about tests in which you have to fill in the blank, answer each question.

1. Fill-in-the-blank tests may have ___clues___ in each sentence that help you figure out the answer.

2. Always plan your ___time___ wisely when taking a test.

3. Should you try to answer every question as soon as you read it? ___No___

4. Should you answer the hard or easy questions first? ___Easy___

5. If you are not sure of a question, you should ___put a mark___ beside it.

Page 62

Preparing For And Taking Tests

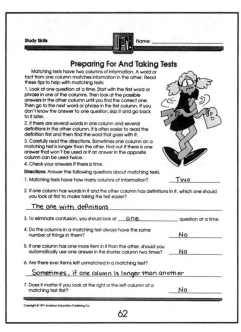

Matching tests have two columns of information. A word or fact from one column matches information in the other. Read these tips to help with matching tests:
1. Look at one question at a time. Start with the first word or phrase in one of the columns. Then look at the possible answers in the other column until you find the correct one. Then go to the next word or phrase in the first column. If you don't know the answer to one question, skip it and go back to it later.
2. If there are several words in one column and several definitions in the other column, it is often easier to read the definition first and then find the word that goes with it.
3. Carefully read the directions. Sometimes one column on a matching test is longer than the other. Find out if there is one answer that won't be used or if an answer can be used twice.
4. Check your answers if there is time.

Directions: Answer the following questions about matching tests.

1. Matching tests have how many columns of information? ___Two___

2. If one column has words in it and the other column has definitions in it, which should you look at first to make taking the test easier?
___The one with definitions___

3. To eliminate confusion, you should look at ___one___ question at a time.

4. Do the columns in a matching test always have the same number of things in them? ___No___

5. If one column has one more item in it than the other, should you automatically use one answer in the shorter column two times? ___No___

6. Are there ever items left unmatched in a matching test?
___Sometimes, if one column is longer than another___

7. Does it matter if you look at the right or the left column of a matching test first? ___No___

Page 63

Preparing For And Taking Tests

Essay questions give you a chance to demonstrate what you have learned. They also provide the opportunity to express your opinion. Although many students think essay questions are the most difficult, they can be the most fun. Remember these tips when writing the answer to an essay question: 1. Think about the answer before you write it. Take time to organize your thoughts so that you can better express yourself. 2. Write a few notes or an outline on a piece of scrap paper or on the back of the test. This helps remind you what you want to write. 3. State answers clearly. Don't forget to use complete sentences. 4. Review the answer before time runs out. Sometimes words are left out. It doesn't take much time to read through your answer to make sure it says what you want it to say.

Directions: Use these essay writing tips to answer the following question in the space provided:

What is your favorite type of test? Give several reasons why.

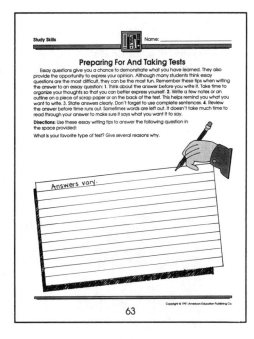

___Answers vary.___

Page 64

Review

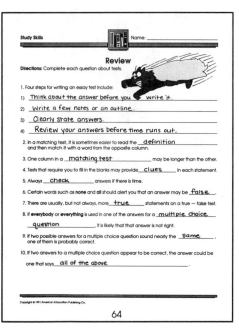

Directions: Complete each question about tests.

1. Four steps for writing an essay test include:
1) ___Think about the answer before you write it.___
2) ___Write a few notes or an outline.___
3) ___Clearly state answers.___
4) ___Review your answers before time runs out.___

2. In a matching test, it is sometimes easier to read the ___definition___ and then match it with a word from the opposite column.

3. One column in a ___matching test___ may be longer than the other.

4. Tests that require you to fill in the blanks may provide ___clues___ in each statement.

5. Always ___check___ answers if there is time.

6. Certain words such as **none** and **all** should alert you that an answer may be ___false___.

7. There are usually, but not always, more ___true___ statements on a true — false test.

8. If **everybody** or **everything** is used in one of the answers for a ___multiple choice___ ___question___, it is likely that that answer is not right.

9. If two possible answers for a multiple choice question sound nearly the ___same___, one of them is probably correct.

10. If two answers to a multiple choice question appear to be correct, the answer could be one that says ___all of the above___.

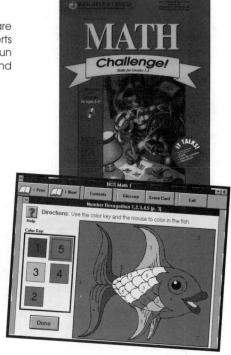

OVERVIEW

ENRICHMENT READING is designed to provide children with practice in reading and to increase students' reading abilities. The program consists of six editions, one each for grades 1 through 6. The major areas of reading instruction--word skills, vocabulary, study skills, comprehension, and literary forms--are covered as appropriate at each level.

ENRICHMENT READING provides a wide range of activities that target a variety of skills in each instructional area. The program is unique because it helps children expand their skills in playful ways with games, puzzles, riddles, contests, and stories. The high-interest activities are informative and fun to do.

Home involvement is important to any child's success in school. *ENRICHMENT READING* is the ideal vehicle for fostering home involvement. Every lesson provides specific opportunities for children to work with a parent, a family member, an adult, or a friend.

AUTHORS

Peggy Kaye, the author of *ENRICHMENT READING*, is also an author of *ENRICHMENT MATH* and the author of two parent/teacher resource books, *Games for Reading* and *Games for Math*. Currently, Ms. Kaye divides her time between writing books and tutoring students in reading and math. She has also taught for ten years in New York City public and private schools.

WRITERS

Timothy J. Baehr is a writer and editor of instructional materials on the elementary, secondary, and college levels. Mr. Baehr has also authored an award-winning column on bicycling and a resource book for writers of educational materials.

Cynthia Benjamin is a writer of reading instructional materials, television scripts, and original stories. Ms. Benjamin has also tutored students in reading at the New York University Reading Institute.

Russell Ginns is a writer and editor of materials for a children's science and nature magazine. Mr. Ginn's speciality is interactive materials, including games, puzzles, and quizzes.

WHY ENRICHMENT READING?

Enrichment and parental involvement are both crucial to children's success in school, and educators recognize the important role work done at home plays in the educational process. Enrichment activities give children opportunities to practice, apply, and expand their reading skills, while encouraging them to think while they read. *ENRICHMENT READING* offers exactly this kind of opportunity. Each lesson focuses on an important reading skill and involves children in active learning. Each lesson will entertain and delight children.

When childen enjoy their lessons and are involved in the activities, they are naturally alert and receptive to learning. They understand more. They remember more. All children enjoy playing games, having contests, and solving puzzles. They like reading interesting stories, amusing stories, jokes, and riddles. Activities such as these get children involved in reading. This is why these kinds of activities form the core of *ENRICHMENT READING.*

Each lesson consists of two parts. Children complete the first part by themselves. The second part is completed together with a family member, an adult, or a friend. *ENRICHMENT READING* activities do not require people at home to teach reading. Instead, the activities involve everyone in enjoyable reading games and interesting language experiences.

NEW! *From the publishers of the acclaimed Master Skills Series*

THE GIFTED CHILD ENRICHMENT READING AND ENRICHMENT MATH FOR GRADES 1-6

An exciting workbook series designed to challenge and motivate children... *the perfect complement to the Master Skills Series!*

ENRICHMENT Reading is designed to provide children with practice in reading and to enrich their reading abilities. The major areas of reading instruction – word skills, vocabulary, study skills, comprehension, and literary forms – are covered as appropriate at each grade level. ENRICHMENT Reading is unique because it helps children expand their skills in playful ways with games, puzzles, riddles, contests, and stories. 64 pages plus answer key. Perfect bound.

ENRICHMENT Math was developed to provide students with additional opportunities to practice and review mathematical concepts and skills and to use these skills at home. Children work individually on the first page of each lesson and then with family members on the second page. At each grade level ENRICHMENT Math covers all of the important topics of the traditional mathematics curriculum. Each lesson is filled with games, puzzles, and other opportunities for exploring mathematical ideas. 64 pages plus answer key.

EACH BOOK IN THE 12 TITLE SERIES INCLUDES:

- 72 pages (64 lesson pages, 8 pg. answer key)
- Table of contents
- Games, puzzles, riddles, and much more!
- Perfect Binding
- Notes to parents
- Additional teaching suggestions
- Perforated pages

Only $4.95 Each!
AMERICAN EDUCATION PUBLISHING
America's Most Innovative Workbook Publisher

150 E. Wilson Bridge Rd. • Columbus, Ohio 43085

ENRICHMENT ANSWER KEY
Reading Grade 6

Page 65 *Missing senses:* sight, taste, touch, hearing; Wording will vary, but answers on the left should focus on smell and memory and answers on the right should focus on the mechanism of smell.

Page 66 Ideas will vary.

Page 67 Summaries will vary, but should tell the basic plot of the story.

Page 68 Comic strips and plot summaries will vary.

Page 69 *Things wrong in picture:* bird flying upside down, weather vane with north, south, east, west reversed, child ice-skating on sidewalk, dog with five legs, thermometer showing 40°, child walking pet dinosaur, sale sign for 120% off, clock with numbers in reverse order, bike floating above ground, snowperson, trash can with "Please Litter" sign, man reading upside-down newspaper, one-way sign pointing in two directions, volcano spouting bubbles, pig driving car, "News" sign with

Page 70 1. F, measured 2. O 3. F, checked a reference 4. F, counted 5. O 6. F, measured 7. F, checked a reference 8. F, counted 9. O 10. F, measured 11. F, counted 12. F, checked a reference 13. O 14. F, measured

Page 71 1. C 2. A 3. B 4. C 5. A

Page 72 1. P 2. E 3. I 4. E; answers will vary

Ellie

Takes a Chance

Zuza Vrbova

Illustrated by Tom Morgan-Jones

CHRYSALIS CHILDREN'S BOOKS

4

Ellie worried a lot, about most things. Lots of things made her feel scared and nervous too. But Ellie made herself feel better by being tidy.

In her bedroom, she liked to arrange all her dresses in neat rows. She liked to spend a long time arranging all her special shells and stones on her shelf.

There were many, MANY things Ellie worried about.

One day, she made a list so that she wouldn't forget any.

Worrying Things

The dark

High places

Spiders

Buttons

Monsters under the bed

Bats

People looking at me,
especially while I am eating

Before Ellie went to sleep, she always checked
under her bed for monsters. Then she arranged
all her shoes — and there were a lot of them —
around the bed as a monster fence.

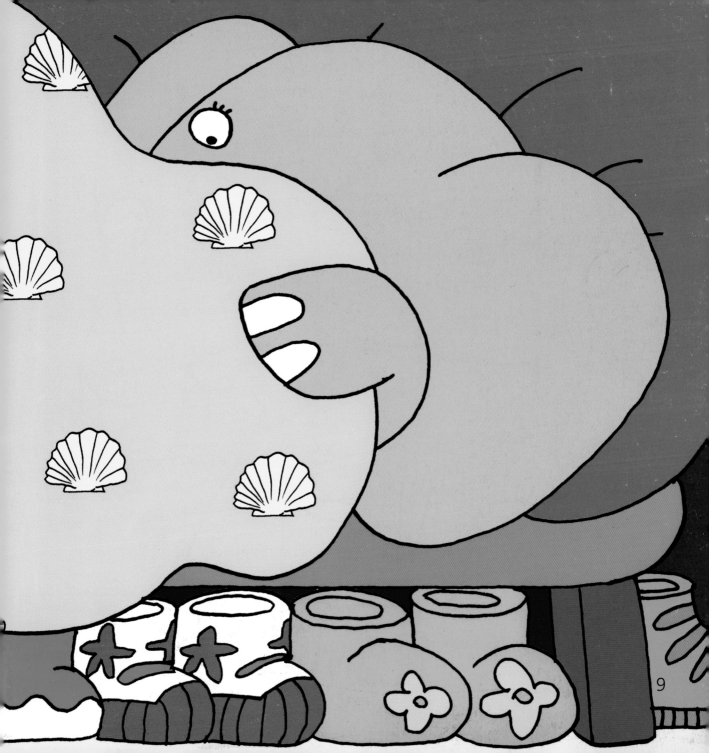

Ellie had a lot of rules for herself, and being tidy
was sometimes hard work. But Ellie always put
her books into a neat pile and her food into
a neat row. (Food was very important to Ellie,
so she liked to keep it tidy.)

The rules are hard, but it is better to stick
to them! she thought.

At school, Miss Roo would ask,

"Is there another word for FAST?"

Or "What is three times three?"

Or "How many seas are there?"

And though Ellie always knew the answer straight away, she never put her hand up. She was shy.

Ellie had one best friend who lived in her pocket. It was a magic pebble. The pebble made sure nothing bad happened to her. Or at least nothing too bad.

One lunchtime, Ellie was having her soup, trying not to make a slurping noise.

"Enjoying your lunch, Ellie?" Crispin said loudly.

Ellie went bright red. Without looking,
she could feel Crispin grinning at her. Everyone
must be looking at her! Ellie reached for
her magic pebble. But her pocket was empty.
The pebble was gone!

After that, everything changed.

When the school bell rang, it bellowed
in her ears. Books thundered onto desks.
Everything sounded louder than before.

And everything looked bigger than before too!

Miss Roo looked like a giant. And Roddy seemed huge!

Ellie breathed hard. What should she do now?

There was only one thing to do.

Ellie curled up behind
the big oak tree and cried.
    Marcus's head peered around
the trunk. "Hey, Ellie, what's up?"
he asked.

"I've lost my magic pebble," sniffed Ellie,

"and now everything is so scary."

    Marcus was Ellie's friend, and he knew

all about the pebble. He thought for a moment.

"Don't worry, Ellie. It can't be really lost.

We'll find it. But in the meantime, I have an idea."

19

Marcus's idea was incredible. "I think you should decide not to be afraid or nervous for one whole day," he said.

"Not afraid of anything?" asked Ellie.

"Not of anything," said Marcus.

"Not even of..." Ellie thought of the scariest, most awful thing she could, "...bats?"

"Not even of bats."

Ellie looked alarmed, but luckily there were no bats around. "But how?" she whispered.

"Easy," Marcus said. "You just make a new rule."

Ellie thought about this for a minute. She was good at making rules. "What rule?" she asked.

"If you are scared about doing something, try to do it anyway," Marcus explained. "You may need to do the opposite to what you normally do."

Ellie wasn't sure about Marcus's idea, but she agreed anyway.

Marcus promised to help.

When Ellie wanted to sit in her usual place
at the back of the class, Marcus suggested,
"Why don't we both sit at the front?"

So Ellie sat at the front, next to Marcus.
It was a little scary, but Marcus was there,
so it wasn't too bad.

When Miss Roo asked, "Which is heavier: a tonne of stones or a tonne of feathers?" Marcus gave Ellie a nudge.

Before she even knew it, she decided to raise her hand. She answered, "They both weigh the same."

"Correct!" said Miss Roo with a smile.

All of a sudden, Miss Roo didn't seem scary at all.

At playtime, when Roddy came by, Ellie reached
into her pocket. But then Marcus winked at her
and whispered, "Remember!"

So Ellie said, "Go away, Roddy," rather boldly. Roddy made a silly face as usual. But Ellie paid no attention and turned and walked away. Roddy went off to pick on someone else.

On the way home, Ellie walked in front of everyone else, rather than behind.

"Marcus," she said, "I had a good day at school today, even though I didn't have my magic pebble."

That night, Ellie didn't arrange her shoes around her bed.
She didn't even check under her bed before she climbed in.
Instead, she made a list of some of the things that
she was no longer scared of:

    Monsters under the bed

    Speaking in class

    Roddy

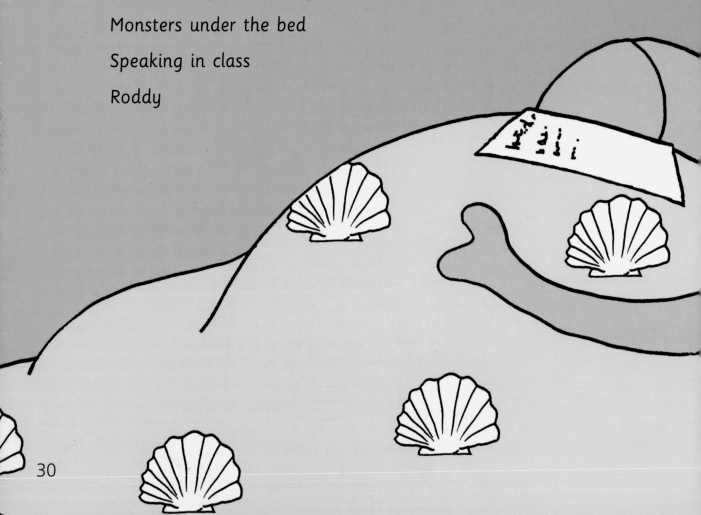

Ellie decided to keep a few things on her list of Worrying Things. I'll deal with Crispin looking at me tomorrow, she thought!

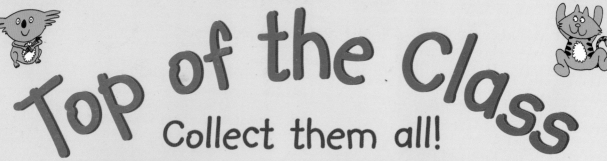

Top of the Class

Collect them all!

Ellie Takes a Chance
1-84458-483-6

Zoë Wins the Race
1-84458-407-0

Piers Finds his Voice
1-84458-406-2

George Makes Friends
1-84458-482-8

Tabby Saves the Day
1-84458-481-X

Kit Paints the Sky
1-84458-404-6

Leo Takes to the Stage
1-84458-405-4

Roddy Learns a Lesson
1-84458-480-1

Visit the Top of the Class website at
www.topoftheclassbooks.com